# HEALING POWER
## OF HORSES

# HEALING POWER OF HORSES

## Lessons from the Lakota Indians

Wendy Beth Baker

Photography by Hope Vinitsky

A Division of BowTie, Inc.
Irvine, California

Karla Austin, Business Operations Manager
Jen Dorsey, Associate Editor
Michelle Martinez, Project Manager
Rebekah Bryant, Editorial Assistant
Erin Kuechenmeister, Production Editor
Ruth Strother, Editor-at-Large
Nick Clemente, Special consultant
Book design and layout by devacommunications.com

This book combines the author's perception of Lakota culture and history with accounts set forth in the bibliography. The author does not consider herself an authority either on the Lakota tribe or on Native Americans as a whole. The Lakota people, whose narratives have been recorded and are completely verifiable, may offer a different account of their history. To avoid repetition, the terms *Native American* and *American Indian* are used interchangeably. The names of all the Special Equestrian Riding Therapy (SERT) students have been changed to protect their privacy.

Permissions to reprint previously published material appear on page 160. Additional photographs courtesy of: ©Roger Wilson, *Burbank Leader*, p. 17; ©Denver Public Library, Western History Collection, pp. 22, 23, 25, 97; Delores Yellow Bull, p 54; Jackie Heathershaw, p.109.

Library of Congress Cataloging-in-Publication Data

Baker, Wendy B.
  The healing power of horses / by Wendy B. Baker.
    p. cm.
  ISBN 1-889540-89-7 (hard cover : alk. paper)
  1. Teton Indians—Domestic animals. 2. Horses—Great Plains—History.
3. Horsemen and horsewomen—Great Plains—History. I. Title.

E99.T34B34 2004
978.004'9752--dc21
                                    2003014033

BowTie Press®
A Division of BowTie, Inc.
3 Burroughs
Irvine, California 92618

Printed and Bound in Singapore
10 9 8 7 6 5 4 3 2 1

In memory of Darwin "Bogie" Carlow.

# Acknowledgments

This book owes its completion to Wayne Waters, Hope Vinitsky, and Nick Clemente; my editors Ruth Strother and Michelle Martinez; and Michael McLaughlin of the American Indian Resource Center at the Huntington Park Library. I also wish to thank everyone who has encouraged me to continue riding: "my hero" Frank LaLoggia, Sandi Kelley, Diane Penders, Dr. Jan Tucker, Dr. Jeffrey Weisel, Nora Fischbach, Ann Berger, Glen Julian, and Nancy Wisler. In addition I'd like to thank the Swicks at Wakpamni Bed & Breakfast; and I especially would like to thank David, my mother and father, and all the exceptional people of the Oglala Lakota Nation: I will always be in your gratitude. *Wopila*.

# Contents

daybreak
appears
when
a horse
neighs

—Brave Bull

# First Words

There are those who feel the sun rises and sets on the back of a horse, and no matter what obstacles life sets in their way, they never dismount. This describes the Oglala Lakota Indians of Pine Ridge, South Dakota.

I am one of those people, too. Despite being some of the best equestrians in the world, the Oglala Indians have had to struggle against poverty and oppression to maintain their relationship with horses. I've had to overcome two physical traumas to continue horseback riding.

The first trauma occurred when I was ten years old and my knees swelled to the size of grapefruits. They hurt all the time. My knuckles swelled, too. Because my family lived in a medical oriented university town, my mother took me to see all sorts of specialists. She even took me to a hospital lecture hall, where I had to take center stage so that interns could ask me questions about my condition. I was finally diagnosed with juvenile rheumatoid arthritis (JRA).

The most humiliating aspect of this condition was that I had to wear corrective shoes to keep my feet from turning in. These clunky outdated shoes were the scourge of my existence. While my classmates were wearing stylish loafers, I hid my shoes by wearing rubbers over them. Despite this, the kids still pointed at my feet and laughed.

So when I wasn't in school, I stayed at home. When my friends were out riding their bikes, playing softball, or taking ballet lessons, I was at home reading. I also wrote short stories because writing was an escape from the physical pain and the loneliness. When my mother bought me a wheelchair, she also bought me a typewriter.

Occasionally, I'd have to be admitted to the hospital for therapeutic treatments. Then, one day after three years, the arthritis mysteriously went into remission. But it left its calling card—my knees had been damaged. To compensate for this, I began riding horses. And since then, I've ridden whenever I've had the opportunity.

The speed, grace, and power of horses give me something I feel the JRA has taken away. When I ride, I experience a state of mind that is like no other. It's an emotion rooted in another part of my being—something basic, primal, spiritual, relaxing, dignifying, unifying (almost like a private religion)—and it can't be replaced by anything else.

After graduating college, I moved to New York City and found my niche in the publishing world. But the stress of the big city took its toll and my arthritis returned. I found a riding stable north of the city, began taking lessons, and never stopped—even after moving to Los Angeles. In fact, horseback riding is more prevalent and accessible in L.A. than in New York. (I like to say it is the only major city in the United States where horse trailers are a common sight on the freeway!)

While in L.A., I bought my first horse. Moonshadow, a 16.1 blue roan quarter horse, was described to me by his former owner as a good "packer," or trail horse. And for several months, it was nothing but bliss between us. Then the second trauma happened.

Moonshadow, a 16.1 blue roan quarter horse, was described to me as a good trail horse.

It was mid-September—a typical Saturday full of errands and housework—and I was fatigued from working all week. But Moonshadow needed to be ridden. By the time my chores were done and Moonshadow was saddled, it was six o'clock. The sun would set around seven, leaving time for an hour's ride.

I was eager to take him to new places. After we successfully completed several exercises on the mountain trails surrounding my home, we made our way along the path by the creek. The sounds of wildlife were beginning to intensify, and Moonshadow was starting to get spooky; he struggled against the reins. I could feel his energy to resist build beneath me, but I pressed on.

Suddenly, a flock of starlings burst out of the reeds, their dark wings beating the air around our heads. Moonshadow took off like a bullet—his black mane flying. We zigzagged along the edge of the creek. I fell off his back, coming down on my hands and knees. There was a loud, sickening crack.

For about thirty minutes I kept trying to get up. I wanted to be like one of those movie cowboys who always recovers immediately. But my right knee had swelled to three times its normal size; my left leg wouldn't move at all; and the ulna bone of my left arm had snapped, making it look like the letter V. Moonshadow was nowhere in sight, and I swore I was going to sell him.

Night settled around me. By the light of a large, white moon, I could see the tall, dry grass I was lying in as well as the reeds lining the bank of the creek, the surrounding sycamore trees, and the craggy peaks of the mountains. The park came alive with chirping and croaking, hooting and howling. Owls. Frogs. Crickets. Coyotes. And some startling noises I couldn't identify. With my one good arm, I grabbed a nearby stick. If a coyote or cougar came near me, I was going to put up one helluva fight. But, mostly, I was just going to lie still and listen and wait. "*Someone* will come for me," I kept saying to myself like a mantra.

Hours ticked by, and I was shivering uncontrollably. My body was in shock, but that protected me from the excruciating pain I should have been feeling. Instead, I felt like I'd had way too much coffee. Every fifteen minutes I checked my watch.

Where was Moonshadow? Finally I heard the clip-clop of hooves and my name being called. I saw the beam of a flashlight scanning the ground.

"Wendy, where are you?" It was my neighbor Frank. He was riding Moonshadow. When he spotted me, he rode down the embankment.

"Frank, I'm hurt real bad." I choked back a sob. It was the first time I'd admitted it to myself, let alone somebody else.

"Don't worry, doll," Frank said. "Everything's going to be okay. I've already called 911."

The police radio crackled in the cold night air and the flashing red light of the ambulance lit up the trees. The emergency rescue team frantically worked above me. They spoke to each other in code. After they placed an inflatable brace around my neck and gently lifted me onto a stretcher, a police officer, pen and paper in hand, asked, "Do you recall what happened?" I did, but I wasn't sure how to explain it to someone who didn't know horses.

I was loaded onto the ambulance and off we went to the hospital. The ride—even with the siren wailing—seemed to take forever. I remember asking if we were almost there; the female paramedic who was sitting by my side told me that we were still in the park!

In the emergency room, the doctors did a good job of keeping me laughing while they poked and probed. But once the X-rays were over and they told me that besides breaking my arm, I had shattered both legs so badly that they needed to be pinned together, I knew my life would never be the same.

A week after surgery, I was transferred to another hospital that specialized in trauma rehabilitation. There I stayed for six weeks, undergoing more surgery and a blood transfusion. The first time I saw the X-rays of the pins in my legs, I went crazy. They weren't the little straight pins I'd imagined. They looked more like a car mechanic's tools—big screws and rods made of titanium that made me look like a robot. I wanted my old body and my old life back so badly that I couldn't stop crying. Finally they sent in a shrink. He wanted to know if I thought my horse felt guilty.

When I returned home in November, I was in a wheelchair. It was impossible for me to get over to Moonshadow's corral. Sometimes I could see his profile from my bedroom window. I obsessed about whether I would ever ride again. When I heard other horses clip-clopping down the street and into the park with their riders, I covered my ears and screamed to numb the pain in my heart. I wished that I had died that night in the park.

My first reunion with Moonshadow came on a cold winter's night. My friend Diane bundled me up in the wheelchair and pushed me down my steep driveway and over rocky ground to his corral. He came to the railing and stared down at me. From my seat, Moonshadow looked even bigger than I remembered. His new winter coat had grown in thick and furry, and his breath shot out of his nostrils in short white puffs. I wasn't mad at him; I didn't miss him. I felt like I didn't even know him. In fact, he scared me.

Our next meeting came a month later, when I was learning how to use a walker. At first I had to set little goals for myself, such as walking from my bed to the window—a huge accomplishment that left me breathless. So it was a big day when I walked from the end of my driveway over to Moonshadow's corral. My steps were slow and small, and walking on uneven ground required leg muscles that I hadn't redeveloped. When I finally made it, I felt like a winner! I clung to the bars of the corral and stood nose-to-nose with Moonshadow for ten idyllic minutes.

For two months, I was overcautious around him, in awe of what his strength and size could do to me. One time, I was leaning on his corral, my walker standing aside on its own. With the tip of his nose, Moonshadow picked up the walker and tossed it aside as though it were a throw pillow. I thought, "That thing is my legs!" and I had to hold onto the bars of the corral to walk over and retrieve it. But, little by little, I became comfortable again in his company. The first time I went *inside* his corral—seven months after the accident, when I was walking with a cane—I longed to climb on his back.

Even after all that I'd been through; there was no question in my mind about wanting to ride again. To me, it seemed as much an obvious next step as walking without assistance. But I wondered if I would be able to ride. One surgeon said that physically I should be capable, but mentally I might not be able to get back on a horse. After all, I'd been through three surgeries, a blood transfusion, and, finally, a total hip replacement. My last surgeon said, "Aren't you a little old to still be crazy about horses?" I answered, "You're my orthopedic surgeon, not my psychotherapist." The best advice came from my internist, who said that if I feel passionate about riding, then I should do it because most people never know what they feel passionate about.

Once I was able to walk without a cane, I brought my western saddle and its wooden stand into the living room and began to sit on it while I watched TV. At first I could stay in the saddle for only thirty seconds, but after a while I worked up to twenty minutes. Now the remaining question was, how was I going to get back up on my horse? One afternoon, my friends Sandi and Diane helped me tack up Moonshadow. Then, while Sandi held his lead rope, Diane helped me climb up a stepladder, lay over his back, and rotate my body forward. I was triumphant! Diane even took a picture, but this was a far cry from actually riding. Then Sandi had a brainstorm. She suggested that I enroll in a program that teaches disabled people how to ride. So, exactly one year after my accident, I went to check out the training center for Special Equestrian Riding Therapy, not knowing that I'd be riding *that* day.

Program Director Nora Fischbach is a caring, no-nonsense woman who knows when to push her students beyond what they think they can do. Nora makes her students feel safe. Her horses are all in their twenties and on the small side. Classes are usually conducted in an arena, with students performing various specially designed exercises. Nora quickly assessed my physical condition, and then led me to a mounting platform that was so high I could sit down on the horse like I would sit down in a chair. Instead of a hard saddle to ride in, there was a woolen bareback pad. Slowly, I swung my leg over the horse's neck. The horse designated for my maiden voyage was a small gray Arabian mare named Kaffeyn, who once belonged to Wayne Newton. I was so terrified of falling off her that I clung to the bareback pad. Two people walked alongside me and another guided the mare with a lead rope. It was not an easy first ride. The hip that I had fractured was killing me whether Kaffeyn stood or walked, and dismounting was so excruciating, it brought four-letter words to my lips. When I finally stood on the ground again—the ride was all of five minutes, but it felt like five hours—Nora gave me a hug and I burst into tears. It had been a long, hard year, and there had been plenty of times when I was afraid I would never ride again.

Despite my difficulties and pain, my disability seemed minor compared to those of my classmates. Alan, a victim of cerebral palsy, struggled to walk with leg braces and two canes, but proudly sat astride his black gelding named King and executed a twenty-meter circle around a barrel. Donna, a twentysomething young lady with Down syndrome, took pride in keeping the tack room orderly when she wasn't riding. And eleven-year-old Bertrand who is an adopted orphan from Rumania had been tied to his crib until the age of seven, causing his feet to deform from disuse. Atop his horse, Sundance, Bertrand recaptured his lost childhood and became a typical, mischievous boy. We all worked together to overcome our impairments, and every Saturday we cheered and applauded each other loudly. I knew there would come a day when I would walk away from this group without my cane; I'd be a stronger and better horsewoman, ready to ride Moonshadow again.

But as hard as I tried to succeed with Moonshadow, it didn't work out. I never got over my fear of him bolting so I was always nervous on his back, which made him nervous. Eventually, I gave him to a more confident rider. Although I can

Mollie and I make a good pair: she has strong legs; I am her sight on the left side.

visit him any time, I've gone only once because it's too emotionally painful to see him.

For about six months after Moonshadow left, I was in "horse limbo"—I had sold my horse property for financial reasons and I wasn't riding at all. In fact, I didn't know if I would ever own another horse. Then I went to a party and met a new friend. The next thing I knew, I was leasing (and am now the owner of) a small Arabian mare. She's sweet, and, like me, she's not perfect. (No living thing is.) Mollie had been blinded in her left eye by a piece of metal roof during a windstorm. She has adjusted to her condition, just as I have adjusted to an artificial hip. I think Mollie and I make a good pair: she has strong legs; I am her eyesight on her left side. Together we are more confident in the arena than out on the trail, but this is a temporary condition. Just as the two eight-inch scars on my left leg and the seven-inch scar on my right leg have faded, so too have the memories of my traumatic accident and difficult recovery begun to fade.

No one can avoid the changes that come from hardships, losses, and pain. In fact, coping with crises is what we struggle with throughout our lives. Picking up the pieces and continuing with life's journey is not easy, and some of us become so obsessed with our problems that we exclude everything else. The result is that we are prevented from moving forward.

Often, we do not open ourselves enough to bond with animals—or with each other—even though bonding is fundamental. Connecting with animals prevents us from becoming species-centric; this, then, increases our empathy with the greater universe. Horses, in particular, help us realize our unity with other living things by reminding us of who we are. They are strong-willed, imposing, and intuitive. We must stay in the moment with them. They invigorate our energy. Training a horse takes patience and heart, not intellect and force. With work and love, we can achieve new heights of self-awareness and feelings by interacting with horses.

Throughout history and in many cultures, horses have played a key role in accompanying individuals on their psychological and/or spiritual quests. In myth and legend, horses have helped people navigate the obstacles within the unconscious parts of their emotional lives and have helped these individuals transmute their imperfections into positive strengths.

One such legend is the story of Standing Bear's horse. In this tale, the enemies of the Lakota have been capturing their horses and running off their buffalo. To solve the problem, Standing Bear asks for volunteers to help him punish the enemies. Ten braves come forward, but as it turns out, Standing Bear is the only one with a horse—and he is a sensitive and intelligent horse, too. So off they go, with Standing Bear riding and the others walking.

After traveling for many days, hunting game along the way, the Lakota catch their enemies and teach them a lesson. Then they begin the long journey home. But while they were away, a terrible grass fire had swept across the plains, and now there isn't any game or grass for man or beast to eat. Soon the braves become weak and tired, and they ask Standing Bear to kill his horse so they can eat. Standing Bear is starving too, but when he looks at his horse standing by submissively, he cannot kill him.

"Give me one more day," he says. "If we don't find food, then tomorrow I'll kill my horse to save your lives." Needless to say, no one finds any food.

The next day the braves eagerly look at Standing Bear's horse, but Standing Bear jumps on his back and rides him to the top of a hill. There he prays to the Great Mystery about his predicament. When Standing Bear opens his eyes, he sees below him in a patch of grass a lone buffalo. Without any prompting, the horse takes off toward the buffalo as if he knows he is saving the braves' lives as well as his own. Standing Bear fires one shot, then another. His prayer is answered, and he races back to the top of the hill, waving his blanket at the braves in celebration.

Such stories are powerful among the Lakota people because they maintain the Lakota's love for horses, which in turn preserves the emotional power of their ancient warrior culture and their strength as a people. By understanding how the horse fits into the minds and hearts of the Lakota, we may discover a model to help us find our way.

Moving westward around the globe,
the horse had at last returned
to the Plains of America—
a unique American odyssey.

—Anonymous

# PART TWO

# The Arrival of Sun'Ka Wakan, the Holy Dog

The horse is a wanderer, just like the Lakota who were once nomads. Before the mid-1700s, there were no horses on the Great Plains. The Lakota had never seen one or heard of one. Then one morning, the Sioux came out of their tepees and there within the circle of their camp were strange-looking beasts feeding on the green grass. They seemed gentle, not heeding the people who stared at them curiously. No one ventured near at first, for the animals were too strange, and no one knew their habits. Everyone stared, but still the animals fed on, scarcely lifting their heads to look at those who began to walk closer for a better view. The head of these strange animals was not shaggy like that of the buffalo; their eyes were large and soft-looking, like those of the deer, and their legs were slender and graceful. A mane flowed from their neck, and their tail reached nearly to the ground. The beauty of this strange animal was greatly praised by first one and then another.

Then, a hunter got a rawhide rope. Maybe these animals would permit being tied, for they seemed so gentle. The rope was thrown toward one of the animals, but he escaped by raising his head on its long slender neck. He raced around a short distance, not in fright nor in anger but as if annoyed. How handsome this animal was when he ran! He did not resemble the buffalo, deer, or wolf, but he was more beautiful than any of them.

The rope was thrown again and again, and at last it was on the animal's neck. He seemed only more kind and gentle and stood tamely while some dared to stroke him gently. Now and then he nibbled grass as if aware he was among friends. Admiration for the lovely animal grew. All wanted to stroke his neck and forehead, and the creature seemed at once to enjoy this extra attention. Finally, a warrior grew brave enough to mount his back. Everyone laughed and shouted with joy! What a wonderful creature! He must have come straight from the Great Mystery, a godsend created by supernatural powers.

A horse who could recover from mortal battle wounds was thought to have supernatural powers.

The Lakota believed that the thunder god, *Wakinyan*, gave the horse to them because the pounding of galloping horses' hooves sounded like thunder. They also thought some horses had more supernatural powers than others. In addition, horses who performed deeds of unusual strength or endurance, who miraculously escaped from battle without a scratch, or who received and recovered from wounds thought to have been mortal, were spoken of as possessing potent secret power.

The people did not know that in later years, this animal would come to them in great numbers and become as great a friend to them as the dog. In time, they would come to think of the

The horse to the Sioux is *Sun'ka Wakan*—Holy Dog.

horse as an inseparable companion in peace and in war, for he faithfully shared the work of the dog, another long-time friend of the Sioux. So to this day, the horse to the Sioux is *Sun'ka Wakan*—Holy Dog.

Once the Lakota became accustomed to the horse, they practiced breeding with remarkable success. The average horse exhibited a wide range of colors and patterns, and as the horse developed on the Great Plains, he acquired amazing speed and stamina.

The Lakota took excellent care of their horses and were knowledgeable about healing herbs. One method of achieving stamina involved blowing pulverized roots or leaves of certain plants up horses' nostrils. The Lakota also sprinkled their fastest horses with cold water daily in the belief that this gave them additional endurance.

Horses became sacred to the Lakota. They were special beings, in the same classification as children and the elderly, containing powers from which they could draw; certainly more meaningful than a mode of transportation. Horses took people not only on external journeys but also on internal journeys to an awareness of feelings and healing, and to the growth of the soul. Horse medicine men had dreams or visions in which they gained knowledge about herbs and roots from wild horses or stallions. With this knowledge, they could not only cure sick horses but people as well.

The horse pervaded the lifestyle, culture, and religion of the Lakota. Horses were used in ceremonies, to transport people, as a medium of exchange, and in battles and gaming. They became second in importance only to the buffalo by giving tribes the ability to hunt widely over the semi-arid Great Plains, control greater territories, and measure a man's worth.

The sound of galloping hooves lead the Lakota to believe that horses came from *Wakinyan*, the thunder god.

Horses were used in ceremonies, gaming, defensive battles, and as a means of exchange.

The horse is sacred to the Lakota, not just a mode of transportation.

# The Sioux Indians

Three tribes make up the Great Sioux Nation. The Ojibwa, who continue to reside in the wooded territories around the Great Lakes, were often in territorial battles with these three tribes, and gave them the derogatory name "Sioux," an abbreviation of the French and Ojibwa word *nadouessioux*, which is generally thought to mean "little snakes."

Years ago the Sioux referred to themselves as the *Oceti Sakowin*, meaning "Seven Council Fires," because they were divided into seven clans, each governed by its own council but all under one confederacy. The clans were at peace with one another except in raids for horses and women. Today, they prefer to be called the Dakota, Nakota, and Lakota. (*Da* means "considered" and *koda* means "friend.") The different names reflect the different dialects, economies, and regions of the *Oceti Sakowin*.

The Dakota, Nakota, and Lakota reside mainly in Minnesota, North and South Dakota, Nebraska, and Montana. The Dakota live to the east, and their economy originally depended on fishing and gathering wild rice. The Nakota are to the southwest, and they once subsisted on the quarrying of pipestone. The Lakota, or People of the Prairie, reside west on the Great Plains; other tribes knew them as the caretakers of the Black Hills. Their economy was based on hunting buffalo and harvesting wild fruits and vegetables such as plums, chokecherries, buffaloberries, and turnips. The three tribes were dependent on one another for survival because each tribe's commerce reflected its locality. They traded with their brethren to provide what the other was lacking.

The Lakota themselves are divided into seven bands. In the early days, when all the bands were present in a formal camp circle, they would sit in the following order: Oglala (Scatter their Own), Minneconjou (Planters by the Water), Sicangu (Burnt Thighs), Oohenunpa (Two Kettles), Itazipacola (No Bows), Sihasapa (Black Feet), and Hunkpapa (End of the Circle). Some of the most notable Lakota historical figures are Crazy Horse and Red Cloud (both Oglala), Big Foot (Minneconjou), and Sitting Bull (Hunkpapa).

A Lakota brave often painted his favorite horse with the same pattern and colors he used on his own face and body, especially when preparing for journeys into enemy territory. A painted horse always carried a message about his rider and sometimes about the quality of the animal bearing the marks.

Horses were painted on both sides, each side telling the same story. Painted symbols included circles around one or both eyes of the horse (to improve the horse's vision) and long zigzag lines symbolizing lightning (adding power and speed to terrify the enemy). These combined symbols were understood to build upon one another, the horse's improved vision giving access to draw upon the lightning's tremendous power. Other symbols included the dragonfly (implying the horse is hard to hit), the lizard (implying the horse is hard to kill), the sacred hoop (showing immortality), the pronghorn antelope (implying swiftness). Golden eagle feathers, still considered sacred, were often tied to the mane and/or tail of a war horse and represented thunder power.

The total effect of a painted brave and his horse was often stunning and made a striking impression upon those who witnessed them.

The symbols painted on a horse tell a story about the rider.

"In this otherwise bleak existence,
a relationship with horses
provides meaning and solace
to those who have them."

# The Lakota Horsepeople of Pine Ridge

The Great Plains has changed only slightly since the Lakota first encountered the horse. There are still prairies that have never been plowed, the short buffalo grass still grips the soil, and the wind blows blustery because of the flat land and the absence of trees. The sky appears large and endless with clouds like horses' tails sweeping across the blue expanse. I know of no other people who love their land or enjoy it more than the Lakota. They love the beautiful streams by which they camp, the trees that shade them, the vast stretches of plains with its fields of sunflowers. The name for the state—dacotah—comes from the Dakota word for "alliance of friends."

The corner of southwest South Dakota has more land diversity than one would think. It's not just the treeless rolling prairie; it also boasts the *Paha Sapa*—the Black Hills—known as "the heart of everything that is." Jagged granite spires are studded with sturdy ponderosa pines. Eighteen peaks reach over 7,000 feet.

Even though the federal government confiscated 7.7 million acres of the Black Hills after miners discovered gold in its gravel-bedded creeks in 1874, the mountains are still the religious and spiritual center for the Lakota.

According to one tribal legend, the Sioux originated underground within the Black Hills themselves. Eventually, they were enticed to the surface of the earth by a wolf who brought food and had been sent as an emissary by Iktomi, the trickster Spider God, at the request of Double Woman. Once they emerged, they were unable to return to the place that had been their home for thousands of years. Their leader, who had been left behind underground, foresaw the fate of his people and the hardships they would encounter. Sacrificing his safe existence, he came to the surface in the form of the buffalo. And it was the buffalo who sustained the people during their early period on earth; this animal provided food, clothing, shelter, tools—all the necessities of life. In fact, the buffalo is still considered today to have all the elements for psychological and physical healing.

More than one hundred years ago, there were three times as many horses as there were people on the land.

Northeast of the Black Hills is the Badlands, an eerie and desolate region of rose-and-cream-colored spires and buttes that the wind and rain have been sculpting for millions of years. The area has hosted strange occurrences: hikers have been known to lose their way in its canyons; three men in a pickup truck accidentally drove over the side of one of its cliffs; a father and daughter were roughhousing on a family outing when the daughter accidentally pushed her father over a ledge; Sheep Mountain Table is supposed to be haunted. Of the 244,000 acres, more than half are on the Pine Ridge Reservation.

The reservation covers 1.2 million acres and supports 30,000 people.

The reservation, surpassed in size only by the Navajo lands, covers 1.2 million acres and supports 30,000 people. Economically, the Pine Ridge Reservation has been deemed the poorest area in the United States, at least in the way such things are measured by white society. The median yearly income is approximately $3,200—less then one-fifth of the national average. Unemployment is nearly 80 percent. There is no industry on the reservation so, as a result, there are few jobs. Many travel 90 to 120 miles to Rapid City to find work. Most of the people who live on the reservation are under eighteen or over sixty-five. The extended family is very important. In a group of aunts, uncles, cousins, brothers, sisters, grandparents, etc., some of the family members have wage-earning jobs, some take care of the children, and others engage in informal trade.

The majority of the Indian people live scattered throughout the countryside in suburban-style housing projects, trailers, log houses, or frame shacks with groups of automobiles parked outside. Most of the homes are some distance away from the main highways, and some are without running water. The people rely on pump

On the Pine Ridge Reservation, buffalo and horses live side by side.

water inspected by the Public Health Service or water from the creek. Some of the homes don't have electricity; kerosene lamps supply light. Nearly all the homes are heated by wood stoves.

The town of Pine Ridge, near the southwest corner of the reservation, is the site of government offices, churches, schools, the hospital, and the seat of the tribal council. There is a grocery store called the Sioux Nation Shopping Center. A nearby Pizza Hut and a Taco John's do bustling business. There's also Big Bat's, a gas station and convenience store. But there is no mall. No movie theater. No motel.

When the Lakota speak of the "good old days," before the domination of white culture, they are referring to the golden age on the Plains—the age of the horse culture. For them, that brief but influential span of glory stands for the good life and has come to symbolize the ideals of freedom and dignity. Horses made this former existence possible and the Lakota were preeminent among Plains tribes for fine horses and skilled horsemanship. It is understandable, then, that they connect to something that is uniquely their own when they relate to horses or participate in equine activities today.

More than one hundred years ago, there were three times as many horses as there were people on the land. Thirty years ago, every Lakota family had horses. Now, only 10 percent of the people on the reservation have horses. One of the reasons for the decrease in the horse population is that many people had to sell their land and move into government housing or to Rapid City for employment. Also, after WWII, the federal government wanted to use the Badlands for a bombing range, so they moved the natives, pushing them into less space. It was ruled that Lakota families could keep only a certain number of horses dependent on their land base. People were then forced to trailer their horses to Rushville, Nebraska, and were compensated a minimum fee for their animals. This was the start of a spiritual and emotional decline. The Lakota turned to alcohol; land use declined; gardens were ignored; white ranchers were given leases for the land. Of the horses now present on the reservation in the early twenty-first century, 1,400 are mares; 1,200 are colts; 300 are geldings, which are used primarily for rodeos; and 150 are stallions.

I have journeyed to the Pine Ridge Reservation three times in four years. I have come to the conclusion that after being confined to the reservation, the Lakota have been strengthened individually and as a community through their relationship with horses. Their connection to the natural world has been kept alive through horses. In this otherwise bleak existence, a relationship with horses provides meaning and solace to those who have them. And from that comes healing and, ultimately, health.

## Wayne Waters

It's four years after my accident. I'm living in California, editing a book on the methods Native Americans use to train horses and I'm loving the project. It gets me wondering about how Indians use horses today compared to long ago. On my way into the office, I happen to pass a Native American gallery that I've never seen before. Even though I'm pressed for time, I decide to stop. When I walk inside, I ask the woman behind the jewelry counter if the store is new.

"No, I've been here for years," she says.

Why hadn't I noticed the gallery before? It's on a main boulevard that I often take. I start to look around. Windspirit Gallery has colorful paintings on the walls, silver jewelry in shiny glass cases, shelves of books for children and adults, and flute music playing in the background. I take my time, not wanting to miss a thing. In the back of the store is an open door that lets in a shaft of strong afternoon sunlight. Next to this door is an Indian man so large that the wooden table and chair at which he sits looks like something fit for a child. He is talking to a conservative-looking woman about the wild horses in South Dakota.

As I eavesdrop, I discover a horse dance stick—the kind of wooden sculpture that Plains Indian warriors used to craft, commemorating the horses they had lost in battle. I pick it up and bring it to the store owner to ask about it; she says that seeing me with it sends chills down her back. So I buy it. The next day, I return to the gallery, hoping to talk to the Indian man about horses. When I pull into the parking lot, he's out front, setting up drums with some other Indian men.

I introduce myself and tell him that I'm interested in how Native Americans work with horses today. Wayne is very receptive and tells me about the many ways horses are used on the Pine Ridge Reservation, where he grew up. It seems they are using the horses for emotional and spiritual healing. At this moment, I know I want to write a book on this subject.

As Wayne speaks, I study his features. His shoulders are as wide as the cement posts in a parking structure. His legs seem as long as two telephone poles. His eyes give him the appearance of being Asian, but his nose is hooked like an eagle's beak and his lips are wide. His thick black hair hangs to his waist, and his arms are brown and smooth. There is no question he is Indian.

When we finish talking, he gives me his card and I welcome the opportunity to stay in touch. After that, we meet several times and speak on the phone about my upcoming trip to the Pine Ridge Reservation and the people I should interview when I'm there. The day before I leave, Wayne calls.

"Would you please look for my horse, Chief, and take his picture so I know he's still alive? He's probably in the Littlefinger's pasture."

I promise him I will.

My two weeks in Pine Ridge are just enough to whet my appetite; I have since fallen in love with the area. The combination of wide-open spaces and warm, generous people (with their quirky sense of humor) is an addictive mix.

One month after I return home, Wayne and I go on a horseback ride in the Santa Monica Mountains, where he gives me details about his life. He talks about being a little boy on the reservation in 1973, when the American Indian Movement occupied Wounded Knee, resulting in a shootout with the FBI. After growing up, he married a traditional Indian girl, whose life was tragically taken by a drunk driver on the day she was to graduate from college. His second wife—of royal Norwegian blood—came to Pine Ridge to study the Lakota culture. They traveled back and forth between the U.S. and Scandinavia; in addition, Wayne took individual journeys to such places as the Middle East. Left alone much of the time, Wayne's wife couldn't adapt to his nomadism. After they divorced, he decided to leave the reservation. A friend drove him to the bus station in Rapid City. One bus was going to California, another to Canada. Wayne flipped a quarter. Heads, he goes to the Golden State; tails takes him north. Heads wins. Wayne climbed aboard the California bus and ended up in L.A., where by some fluky chance (call it horses bringing people together) we met.

Wayne goes on to spend four years in L.A., making jewelry, lecturing at schools, gardening, painting houses, and doing just about anything else he can to earn a little cash. Now, he's on the road again. Sometimes, he calls from northern California; other times, from Oregon or Arizona. He says he's going to move to Nevada. But no matter where he is, Wayne is still the nomadic Indian of the Great Plains. And he is still lonesome for Chief.

## Postscript —

When Wayne and I first met, we were both somewhat adrift and emotionally and spiritually lost. My marriage was slowly disintegrating. The accident had taken its

---

No matter where Wayne lives, he is still the nomadic Indian of the Great Plains.

toll on my then-husband because of the demands it put on him, and he had retreated into his own private world. Without any intimacy between us, and because I still was not the rider I once had been, I had become physically lost.

Meanwhile, Wayne was searching for his socioeconomic place off the reservation. He wanted to see where he fit in a world in which he was a minority with a philosophy about the earth and animals that was different from the cultural norms. Even though there was little prejudice against Native Americans in California, Wayne was cautious and unsure of himself. But I was drawn to his inner strength as dewdrops are drawn to a blade of grass.

When we are together, we nourish each other with stories about horses; mainly Wayne reminisces about Chief and I about Moonshadow. We remember the days when we felt free and boundless. It is our high, our mutual escape from the struggle of our daily lives.

# Marlin "Moon" Weston

Nicknamed after Moon Mullins, the 1920s cartoon character, Marlin "Moon" Weston is anything but comical. At the age of 36, he is a devoted husband and father and the owner of a profitable horse-breeding business. And that's not all. He also has the distinguished title of Tribal Council representative for the Oglala Lakota Nation in the Porcupine District of the Pine Ridge Indian Reservation.

The walls of Moon Weston's comfortable home are covered with photographs of him and his wife, the two bronco bulls who made it to the National Rodeo Finals, and his grandfather on horseback. His most prized photo is one taken of Barbara Bush presenting him with the Maxwell House Real Heroes of America Award for bringing handicapped ramps, railings, extrawide doors, lavatories, and reserved parking places to Pine Ridge. Until he formed the Quadriplegic Squad or Quad Squad as it is more commonly known, disabled people on the reservation were confined to their homes. But before Moon achieved any of these accomplishments, a tragic accident changed the course of his life.

It is 1983, and Moon's spirits are high. Married eleven months to his high school sweetheart, Evie, the two are expecting their first child. One day in July, he and his friend Popcorn are driving back to Porcupine, South Dakota, from Pine Ridge. They have been riding young bulls all day long, and they are tired and sore. Popcorn falls asleep at the wheel. The car, a Chevy Nova, rolls into a ditch and Moon is thrown 300 feet; his neck is broken. The rest of that summer night is a blur as he goes in and out of consciousness, blood pouring from his ears and nose. All he knows is that he has to be airlifted to a hospital in Denver, where a special surgeon is waiting to operate.

As Evie is giving birth to a baby boy in Rapid City, Moon is undergoing surgery in Denver; the rest of the family is shuttling back and forth between the two, trying to keep things in order. But only so much can be done for a spinal cord injury of the sixth cervical vertebrae. The fact is that if any of the eight cervical vertebrae in the neck is injured, the result is usually a loss of function in the arms and legs (quadriplegia). Fortunately, Moon is considered an incomplete quadriplegic because he can use his wrists and he has enough hand function to feed himself and drive his truck. But he won't walk again. To symbolize the delicate balance between life and death, he and Evie name their only son Chance.

Ranching, Moon's livelihood, is taken away from him. Before the accident, he was on horseback so much that he seemed like a centaur. Afterward, Moon's friends invite him to watch them play basketball, thinking that would lift his spirits when, in effect, all it does is stir up anger and resentment. "People don't realize how tough it is to get up every morning and get into a wheelchair. Or to have your wheelchair get stuck in the mud when you're trying to go someplace."

Moon, Evie, and Scott thrive on being with their horses and each other.

It takes Moon two years to accept the fact that he is never going to walk again. One of the ways he overcomes his anger and depression is by going out to his field of horses to watch them and be in their company. Moon doesn't focus on one specific horse to lift his spirits because ever since he lost a favorite horse in boyhood, he has vowed never to get that close to one again. However, just being near all his horses keeps him going.

Horses not only take people on external journeys but on internal journeys as well. They bring us to a new awareness of feeling and healing and help our souls grow. Since horses are strong and quick, they force us to stay in the moment with them instead of focusing our attention on ourselves to the exclusion of everything else. They invigorate us, which leads to our desire to be alive. By watching his horses, Moon was rebuilding his psyche and his body. He reveres the horse for its power, speed, and grace. Horses are the epitome of movement; the antithesis of the life of a quadriplegic.

After Moon begins to heal, he starts the Quad Squad, making countless phone calls to various agencies to get the funding necessary to bring disabled facilities to Pine Ridge. Then he begins his horse-breeding business. "I don't want people to pity me. I've accomplished more in my lifetime than I ever thought was possible. People can do anything they set their mind to."

When I first meet Moon on a warm Sunday afternoon, he is sitting on the front porch of his parents' home. A mutual friend tells me to look for a tall Indian, and I wonder how someone in a wheelchair can be described as tall. But when I meet Moon, I understand. He sits up very straight and proud in his chair, and he looks at me directly, holding eye contact for a beat or two longer than most people do.

On his 960 acres of land, Moon has forty horses that he uses for breeding. Evie drives us to the pasture where he keeps the mares and foals and a herd of paints in every color and pattern imaginable. They look like a crazy quilt, embedded in grass knee-deep in a grove of fir trees on the side of a hill. Many of them have blue

Every mare has a yearling beside her who is a reflection of herself.

eyes. "To make a horse that everyone wants is a challenge. I like to breed for color, conformation, and size. Team ropers are my best customers."

As Moon; Evie; Chance; Moon's brother, Scott; and I approach, the horses scatter in all directions. They're not used to seeing so many people at once! But Scott brings a bucket of sweet feed. With palms extended, we offer them mounds of sticky yellow oats. We quickly become their friends.

Every mare has a pint-sized yearling beside her who is a miniature version of her. The yearlings hide in their mother's shadow and won't let us get near them, no matter what we are giving away. One little palomino looks as if she has just come from having a perm at the beauty parlor: all of her hair is curly! (Later, I learn that there is a Lakota pictograph from the winter of 1800–01 depicting the capture of one of these curly-haired horses. The Lakota believed such hair had been singed, hence the name *sung-gu-gu-la*, or "horse with burnt hair.") While we're admiring her, the alpha mare suddenly decides to move the herd. They all take off at once, and we have to move quickly out of the way. This happens again and again over the course of the day and keeps us entertained.

The next time I see Moon, he's been reelected as Porcupine Tribal Council representative. It's his fourth term in office. He also mentions an upcoming Ride for Life in which the people of Pine Ridge ride their horses in memory of those killed in automobile accidents. Evie is keeping busy, running the diabetes program at Pine Ridge Hospital. Chance is in high school, and Moon is hoping that his son will follow in his footsteps and become a team roper and rodeo rider. Right now, though, Chance is more interested in football and basketball. And the horse-breeding business is going well. Sixteen mares will give birth in the spring.

## Postscript—

Because of the limitations on my ability to move—imposed upon me by juvenile rheumatoid arthritis and later by my accident—I have idealized horses because their movements seem free. As a child, I often felt that I would become agile and lithe if I could learn to ride and participate in their movements. Moon's restricted movement came later in his life than did mine. He was already an accomplished horseman when his life drastically changed. Since his accident, he, too, has been able to recover some of the pleasures of movement by visually enjoying his horses and participating in their lives as a horse breeder.

His hope that Chance may someday build an identity and a life centered around horses is like a second chance for Moon to ride again, although vicariously. I am lucky to have been able to relearn how to ride and to overcome the trauma of my riding accident. I guess I've had a different sort of chance.

# Eugenio White Hawk

I meet Eugenio at the police station, located past the Crazy Horse Housing off Hwy 407. He's a cop and has just finished his overnight shift. Things are busy at the station this morning with talk of some horse thieving going on.

Horse raiding began during the golden age of the Plains Indians (1750–1886), when the Sioux and other tribes learned the value of the animal. Running off the enemies' horses was considered legitimate and honorable, like going to battle. The Sioux likened it to capturing, not stealing, and looked upon the act as an example of cunning and craftiness, a robust and manly pastime, a training in the virtues of patience and courage. The young man who excelled in it became a hero among his peers and/or tribe.

Dozens or more young men would constitute a raiding party. The adventure could take days, months, even a year and was done in any season. (In winter, the horses wore white hoods and blankets as camouflage.) Sometimes, the leader carried medicine that would either tranquilize the enemy or cause weather conditions that prohibited the enemy from giving chase. Raiding was a thrilling activity for young men. Early examples of kleptomania and schizophrenia resulted from this activity because of its addictive thrill. One young man was deluded into thinking his raiding buddies had turned into horses, and he insisted that they all whinny! Another fellow's uncontrollable urge led him to steal horses from his own tribe. But today, horse thieving is no longer looked upon with admiration.

Eugenio's wife, Denise, is assisting the police by rounding up and loading the stolen horses (a palomino mare and yearling) into the family's horse trailer. Before I interview Eugenio, I follow him in his van to Pinky's grocery store in Manderson, where we meet up with Denise in the parking lot. From there, we go to Eugenio and Denise's home, tucked way back in the hills at the end of a dirt road. There's a lot of land, most of it open space. Sage, sunflowers, and purple bee plant clog the road and horses are running free all over the yard. Four kids ranging in age from ten to fifteen—Tyler, Grace, Jessie Luke, and Marietta—come out to greet me.

Denise makes a pitcher of ice water and we sit in the shade in the backyard. Right next to us in a rabbit pen, a mother rabbit has given birth to seven baby bunnies. My gifts sit on the table, still wrapped, being explored by four pairs of curious hands.

Eugenio tells me that the horse is still considered sacred today. There's a saying that if you do anything to harm a horse, the same thing will happen to you. Because of the role the horse has played in Lakota culture (tribal warfare, horse raids, property), it belongs more to the man than to the woman. In fact, Lakota believe that women shouldn't ride during their menstrual cycle because they're "not clean."

Suddenly, our conversation is interrupted when more kids arrive—a whole parcel of boys, including one with glasses and neck-length hair nicknamed Cowboy. Typical teenagers, they strut, spit, and show off, but they pay Eugenio respect and listen to what he says. "Get the horses ready," he commands. It's time for the games.

A small orange kitten follows us into the field. Eugenio pairs everyone up for five different races. He goes over the rules and then, just before he waves the horses away to give the riders a good running start, he bestows a special tip to each rider. All the events are timed; it's my job to watch the clock. I keep track of the scores by watching the second hand of my watch. The boys have some good times.

"What was your best time?" I ask one.

"This time," he says. The kids enjoy playing with the double meaning of our words.

Riding at Eugenio's is a happy occasion.

# The Races

Back-to-Back Race: Pairs ride double on a horse, with the person in the back facing away from the one sitting in the saddle.

Boot Race: All the riders gallop to the end of the field, dismount, put on a rubber boot, get back in the saddle, and return to the starting line.

# The Races

Hide Race: A rider pulls someone behind him on the ground. This person is lying on whatever can be found in the yard such as a piece of plastic, canvas, tarp, sled, or saucer.

Rescue Race: One rider swings another rider up behind him as he makes the turn to come back toward the finish line.

Later, at the powwow and rodeo grounds, I see Eugenio on horseback and in uniform with Oglala Lakota Nation Police printed on the back. All the policemen are carrying guns, but the partnership of horse and rider conveys such an impression of authority and control that guns seem unnecessary. The policemen and their mounts are imposing because you can see them from far away; conversely, they can overlook the grounds from a distance, thereby evoking a sense of security. The power of the policeman on his horse further hints of the conquest of man over untamed beast.

## Postscript—

Through horses, Eugenio is able to maintain a bond with his sons and their friends as well as be a positive role model for them. Horses also unite him to the community and strengthen his self-image. When he engages in activities in uniform and on horseback, he becomes more than a cop. The traditional image of the Lakota male combines with the authority of the policeman to facilitate acceptance of the law. It's especially important that young people respond to him positively in his role as a cop since many of his duties involve working with kids.

Likewise, feeling accomplished as a horsewoman and having friends in the horse community help my self-esteem. I feel as though I am accepted unconditionally without having to prove myself; I am part of a special family. It also has enhanced my relationship and sense of continuity with my mother and my Aunt Nancy, who both used to ride and who equally appreciate a more rural culture, just as I do.

A Lakota policeman on his Lakota horse.

## Wendell Yellow Bull

Alcoholism on the reservation is a painful and complicated subject to discuss. However, driving through Whiteclay, Nebraska—the town nearest the reservation where one can buy liquor—anyone can see that alcoholism among Indians is no better now than it was before current public awareness or existing social programs came to be. The Indians still are suffering from unresolved feelings of grief over their historical losses and generational traumas, such as Wounded Knee I and II, repeated illegal seizures of their lands, the shortage of jobs, and chronic poverty.

As you enter Whiteclay driving north on Highway 87, a traffic sign orders you to slow down to 35 mph, and it's important that you do. Although Whiteclay is only about three blocks long and easy to miss, there are so many drunks crossing

Following the Sobriety Ride, the powwow dancing begins.

the road in the bleached-white heat of the afternoon that you are likely to hit some-one. You might see one or two women, but most of them are middle-aged men. Sometimes they're standing in a circle arguing; sometimes they're lovingly wrapped in each other's arms underneath a shady tree; there is usually someone sitting off by himself, his head in his hands. You'll see a lot of dogs lolling about as if they, too, are hungover. According to *Indian Country Today*, the four liquor stores in Whiteclay sell more than eleven thousand cans of beer each day, mostly to the residents of the Pine Ridge Indian Reservation.

To combat this problem, the Lakota have created the Sobriety Rides. On the first day of the Sixteenth Annual Oglala Lakota Nation Powwow and Rodeo, sixty-five Sobriety Riders, men and women both, arrive at the fairgrounds in Pine Ridge. They have been riding horses for four days, covering 70 miles, camping along the way.

After riding for four days, the Sobriety Riders reach the fairgrounds.

Many young men participate in the Sobriety Rides just to feel connected to the tribe.

Elders pass on the experience of riding to their young.

After they make their grand entry in the arena, they rest their wobbly legs by corralling their horses into a nearby field. Nobody wants to get back in the saddle for a while.

With heartfelt anticipation, a dancer watches the riders approach.

Wearing wire-rimmed glasses, Wendell Yellow Bull, one of the lead riders, sits in his folding canvas chair as though he's presiding over a herd of buffalo; he seems all-knowing and all-seeing. I introduce myself and we talk about how horses have helped the lives of Lakota Indians. He studies me for a while, then gets up and leaves. A chow line is forming, a dinner in memory of Tribal Council member Darwin "Bogie" Carlow, who was very active in organizing the kids' rodeo. People invite me to get some food and eat, but I do the polite "white thing" and respond, "No thank you," not realizing I made a huge Indian faux pas: one never refuses an offer of food.

When Wendell returns, he tells me that Sobriety Rides began as an offshoot of the Big Foot Memorial Ride: the Lakota take to riding to make a clean break from a life of drinking and taking drugs. The activities of the riders are always announced on KILI, the Voice of the Lakota Nation, and flyers are passed out in the community. Typically there's a ride late in July, before the Oglala Lakota Nation Powwow and Rodeo. Because camping and the use of pack horses are involved, a ride often takes three months of planning in which about five thousand dollars needs to be raised. The rides usually last two to five days and start off with twenty-five to thirty-five riders. By the final days, the number of riders increases to as many as 100 or 150. The rides cover 100 miles across the Pine Ridge Reservation.

Sometimes entire families participate, but usually more men than women ride, and the age range is typically fourteen through thirty-five—the time of life when people are most likely to get involved with drugs and alcohol. Many young men participate for the joy of the ride. Others may ride to reconnect with their spirituality, Lakota culture, language, and horses. They don't have to have their own horse or even be experienced riders. Some families donate horses to those going on their first trail ride.

Prior to the ride, the horses are decorated with eagle feathers and smudged with sage and cedar. This symbolizes the connection between the rider and the

The fury and passion of ceremonial dancing reconnects the Lakota to their heroic past.

horse and brings good feelings and thoughts during the ride. Before the riders head out, they sing both traditional and newly created songs and say prayers of remembrance to venerate the horses and the journey. Scouts are selected, and people are assigned various responsibilities, such as to look after the kids.

Every day thereafter, both the riders and horses are smudged with more sage, and more songs are sung and more prayers are said. Then the scouts, followed by the rider who carries the staff, ride in a clockwise circle (as the sun rises and sets) to signify their unity, that they are going forth as one, as the other riders continue to sing songs. During the ride, elders share old Lakota stories. Sometimes these stories have a profound effect on a rider who has taken up self-destructive habits and who is trying to straighten out. Many of the horses are given a special name at some point during the ride. Then more stories and food are shared at the end of the day.

Sobriety Rides are beneficial to the individual riders and to the community as a whole, and probably more of them would be organized were it not for the money and time necessary to produce them. Although it's true that any organized activity that draws the community together offers positive effects, the presence of and interaction with the horse is more traditional to the Lakota culture and therefore more sustaining. Mel Lone Hill, another rider, tells me that some of the older people on the reservation who used to participate in Sobriety Rides have since lost their connection with horses and have gone back to drinking.

As a next step, I learn from Wendell in our last conversation that he has recently established a nonprofit organization called *Sun'ka Wakan na Waknyeja Awicaglipi*, which means To Bring Back the Horse and Child. Its purpose is to teach the Lakota perspective of horsemanship, leadership, and wilderness training to the youth of the community. Equally as important, the organization will strive to keep the Lakota language alive.

Lakota say prayers of remembrance to venerate the horses and the journey.

# Postscript —

When Wendell asked me what I had learned about Lakota horsepeople, I told him that I think they experience the same benefits from horses that I do. I would rather ride Mollie than have a glass of wine.

When I ride, I have to be so focused on my horse that I can escape from everyday pressures and completely relax. It's a narcotic of sorts because it provides relief from everyday problems while at the same time it forces a rider away from being intoxicated because it demands mental discipline. A horse needs her rider to be the leader and can sense when her rider isn't alert. This could lead to a dangerous situation. A mind that is clouded by drugs or alcohol is slow to respond to a horse's signals. Horse and rider must learn to trust one another for the relationship to work and for that trust to occur there must be a flow of clear, unobstructed communication.

# Aldeen Twiss, Phillip Jumping Eagle, and his brother, Billy

Aldeen Twiss is the great-granddaughter of Captain Thomas Twiss, who was the Indian agent for the Great Sioux Nation from 1855 to 1861. Captain Twiss graduated second in his class from West Point Military Academy. During his duty in the Dakota Territory, he became sympathetic to the Indians and married an Oglala woman named Lightning Shield, who later came to be called Mary. Twiss acted as an ombudsman between the Indians and the whites and was instrumental in facilitating trade, including the trade of horses. When he died in the early 1870s, Mary and their seven children rejoined the Oglalas at the Red Cloud Agency on what is now the Pine Ridge Indian Reservation. Aldeen's mother, who was Mary's granddaughter, had thirteen children.

Aldeen grew up on horseback. She recalls the high-speed riding she did with her brothers.

"Hurry up, you wimp!" they'd say.

"I ain't riding no more with you guys! You go too fast."

"Stop whining and hang on!"

And away they would go, galloping down hills and across the grassy plains. When Aldeen would finally dismount, she could barely walk. "I was a virgin until I got on those horses!" she exclaims.

There was a time when Aldeen Twiss spent her money on liquor and gasoline: one fueled her, the other fueled her car. She has been married six times and has either five or six kids—she can't remember which. Because she was always out carousing, her children were taken away from her. About five feet tall, she has long straight chestnut hair and acorn-colored skin, warm brown eyes, and the Lakota profile. She's most striking when she wears royal blue.

When we jump ahead to 1984, Aldeen is no longer drinking and she has settled down with Phillip Jumping Eagle. Their place is on Indian Service Road 27 just outside of Manderson. Aldeen helps take care of the horses, Shetland ponies, and eight buffalo who occupy their 320 acres. And she is a cook at Manderson Elementary School. This keeps her plenty busy; I know, for she's always out of breath when I reach her on the phone.

*Rrnngg! Rrnngg!*

"Hi, Aldeen! What are you doing?"

"I just got in from feeding the buffalo. It's freezing out, and they wouldn't let me in the gate, so I had to wait until they wandered off, and then when they saw me come inside the fence with their bowl, they charged me! I had to throw that bowl down and run like hell! I hope no one was watching me—they would've laughed."

Aldeen and Phillip's home is within a little cluster of trailers on land that stretches out like the sea. Up the hill from them lives Billy, Phillip's younger brother. He has two draft horses—giant Percherons, to be exact. Percherons stand up to 19 hands high and can weigh up to 2,600 pounds. Their hooves are the size

Aldeen and Phillip's buffalo feeding with its baby.

of dinner plates! Most often they are black or gray, but you'll also see sorrels, bays, and roans. Billy has bays.

Before seeing these horses, I did a little research on the breed and found that the Percheron is considered to be the most elegant of the heavy draft horses. One nineteenth century author described it as an Arab influenced by climate and agricultural work; indeed, Arabian stallions did sire some of the most famous Percherons.

The name *Percheron* comes from the place that serves as its cradle—Le Perche—a historical region of France. There, the horses were so accustomed to affectionate attention that docility became one of their inherited traits. In their long history, the Percheron has been a warhorse, coach horse, farm horse, and heavy-artillery horse. In fact, thousands of Percherons served on the battlefields of the First World War.

When Billy purchased his Percherons, they had never been hitched to a wagon. As soon as Billy harnessed them and climbed into the wagon seat, they took off and jumped over a washing machine, dragging the wagon behind them like a woolen muffler. Billy was thrown into the wagon bed, where he lay prostrate, saying his prayers.

Billy's Percherons aren't used for farm work. They have been assigned a special duty within the community: at funerals, Billy's Percherons pull the caskets from the church to the cemetery, while horseback riders follow behind the wagon singing the old Lakota "Riders' Song" about the sacredness of horses and their riders.

This function took on a much larger significance for Billy when the Native American Graves Protection and Repatriation Act was passed in 1988. This act requires museums to inform tribes if they have any tribal artifacts or ancestral

Billy's Percherons pull caskets from the church to the cemetery during funerals.

# Indian Burial Grounds

Collecting Indian body parts was official government policy from 1867 to 1868. The U.S. Surgeon General issued orders for army personnel to obtain Indian skulls for study at the Army Medical Museum in Washington, D.C. The 1868 order stated, "While exotic and normal and abnormal crania of all descriptions are valued at the Museum for purposes of comparison, it is chiefly desired to procure a sufficiently large series of adult crania of the principal Indian tribes to furnish accurate average measurements."

This policy required the desecration of thousands of graves and the pillaging of hundreds of battlefields—all in the name of science. But, of course, the Surgeon General wasn't employing grave robbers; he was using "collectors." And if there was any doubt about the value and righteousness of the task, one collector, Army Surgeon Z.T. Daniel, offered this account of his undertaking in a letter written in 1892:

"I collected them in a way somewhat unusual: the burial place is in plain sight of many Indian houses and very near frequented roads. I had to visit the country at night when not even the dogs were stirring. After securing one skull, I had to pass the Indian sentry at the stockade gate, which I never attempted with more than one skull for fear of detection.

"On stormy nights, I think I never was observed coming or going by either Indians or dogs, but on pleasant nights, I was always seen; but of course no one knew what I had under my coat. The greatest fear I had was that some Indian would miss the heads, see my tracks, and ambush me. But they didn't."

Essentially, the army surgeon was digging up Indian bodies, cutting off the heads, and slinking away under the cover of night with the skull in tow. Some remains were stolen from scaffolds; other skulls were taken from Indians who had been captured and executed by the U.S. government.

remains so they can make the necessary arrangements to bring the pieces home.

In 1998, a train pulled into Omaha, Nebraska, loaded with boxes of bones, which were then transported by truck to Pine Ridge. With great care and respect, Phillip Jumping Eagle loaded the cardboard boxes into the back of Billy's wagon. Quietly, the Percherons awaited their cue to start the journey. When it was time, many of the onlookers who had gathered for the occasion began to weep. Billy then took the remains to the Sioux Funeral Home, where descendants could claim their ancestors.

When I first visited Aldeen and Phillip, the entire Jumping Eagle clan and their neighbors came down the hill to greet me. Besides Billy there's his wife, Donna; her beautiful daughter, Sarita, and Sarita's two children, five-year-old Roger Big Boy, and one-and-a-half-year-old Sarah; there is also Cousin George Looks Twice, a devout Christian; and the neighbor Rueben Yellow Thunder, soft-spoken, with short-cropped hair and a baseball cap.

The Jumping Eagle clan and their neighbors.

We gathered around a picnic table in the front yard for an outdoor feast of ham hocks and pigs' feet stewed in hominy, along with corn on the cob, and *wojapi* (raspberry pudding). All the dishes were prepared by Phillip, whose hobby is watch-

ing whatever cooking shows his satellite dish can bring in on the TV. As we line up for second helpings, dark clouds form and the sky threatens rain. No one seems to mind. The Jumping Eagles were anxious to talk about their lives. They told me about a two-day reservation ride they had organized to honor children and teach them to respect themselves. More than a hundred riders participated.

One of Aldeen's beaded saddle blankets.

When the meal was over, we took pictures of everyone around the wagon. Then Billy hitched up the horses, and I was treated to a demonstration of wagon-pulling over bumpy terrain. Billy flew behind the horses like Santa in his sleigh.

Hours later, Aldeen, Phillip, and I sat in the living room, listening to the patter on the roof. There appeared to be a leak in the kitchen ceiling and I mentioned this, trying to be helpful. My observation was met with a shrug, leaving me more embarrassed about pointing out the flaw than Phillip and Aldeen were about having it. As we chatted, Aldeen was beading. She showed me some of her latest work, including a beaded blue-and-white saddle blanket. She sews the sparkling beads onto canvas, or sometimes leather (yes, it's hard on your fingertips), at the rate of a half inch per three hours, and then she uses a trade blanket as backing. This project took her two years to complete. It was used once in a parade.

Before I left for the evening, Aldeen ventured out into the storm to get me some fresh, warm Indian fry bread, made by an elderly woman who lives down the two-lane paved road. By this time, the roads were so bad that I wondered if I would be able to make it back out to the highway.

As I drove the stormy miles back to my motel, I try tried to picture the Dakota Territory in 1855, and what Captain Twiss experienced when meeting the Sioux for the first time. Did he have to offer his wife's father many fine horses to win the daughter's hand in marriage, as was the custom back then?

Then, I passed Wounded Knee and thought of all the people who had been massacred or had died in battle, their heads confiscated and studied like quaint artifacts by our nation's capital. I also thought of the horses who carried the soldiers to battle. A hundred years later, when justice is finally served and the ancestral remains are returned, it is horses who carry them home.

# The Bones of a Horse

> Look back at our struggle for freedom,
> *Trace our present day's strength to its source;*
> *And you'll find that our pathway to glory*
> *Is strewn with the bones of a horse.*
>
> —*Anonymous*

---

## Postscript—

Aldeen's life with the Jumping Eagles has helped her resolve a difficult young adulthood. The ritualized horse activities have provided structure to a somewhat disorganized, chaotic identity. She has gone through stages in her life when she was unable to establish stable, long-term relationships or a sense of responsibility for her children. However, maintaining her horses and buffalo has served as her model for responsible behavior toward people. Her adult life has been better for it.

Billy's involvement in the care of Lakota ancestral remains by means of his horses psychologically anchors him to his people. This, in turn, provides him with an alternative source of dignity and status, which, in more affluent cultures, people get from their professions and careers. He is the semiofficial bearer of ancestral remains and is recognized as such by the rest of the community.

I've had my own chaotic times and didn't always have horses to root me. Since I've acquired a horse of my own, I've become calmer and less preoccupied with my problems. This has enabled me to reestablish my family ties, which were once strained when I was figuring out who I was. My horsewomanship doesn't occur in a vacuum, but is woven into all of my other relationships. People who know me know the importance of horses in my life, and I share with them stories about my activities with Mollie. I believe this has changed the way they view me, and I receive a type of recognition and support that goes beyond the gratifications that I obtain from my career.

# (He's an) Indian Cowboy

Sun is up,
Day is on
Look for me,
I'll be gone
cuz today's the day
I'm gonna see
him again

He's an Indian cowboy
in the rodeo
and I'm just another little girl
who loves him so
He's an Indian cowboy
in the rodeo
and I'm just another little girl
who loves him so

Once he stopped
and talked to me
I found out
how dreams can be
with a big wide smile
and a big white hat

He's an Indian cowboy
in the rodeo
and I'm just another little girl
who loves him so
He's an Indian cowboy
in the rodeo
and I'm just another little girl
who loves him so.

—Buffy Sainte-Marie

## Dale Vocu

It's 107 degrees at the Oglala Lakota Nation Powwow and Rodeo. Outside the rodeo grounds, dozens of pickup trucks and horse trailers are parked every which way, with horses tied to trailer bars waiting for their events. Someone brings his baby goat and leaves the animal tied to his front bumper. The owners are not around, so I fill a plastic feed bucket with water and feed him saltines. Indian cowboys and cowgirls are loping in the field, while kids of all different sizes and shapes are tearing up the dirt road on their ponies. The hot, dry Dakota wind kicks up the dust and swirls it around the ponies legs. In the grandstands, people are sitting under blue tarps and striped beach umbrellas, holding bottled water to their foreheads to keep cool. The lemonade stand is doing a record business.

The rodeo begins with A Cowboy's Prayer. Rodeo officials sit astride their horses and line up inside the arena while the prayer is read over the loudspeaker. Some of them hold their cowboy hats over their hearts while several women beneath the announcer's stand hold up a handmade star quilt as an honorary backdrop.

"How we doin' out there? Are we having a good time, Oglala?"

*Whistles, clapping, shouts.*

"Our first rider comin' up is Jeremy Meeks, from Interior, South Dakota. A saddle bronc rider, a bareback rider, and a good one—you bet! He ended up second in the all-around with a 78. [out of 100] ride. All right, let's sell him."

After the audience hears this remark, they know it's time to start betting on the rider. The announcer runs it like an auction. "Somebody give me twenty-five, twenty-five, twenty-five, lookin' for twenty-five, yeah! Now fifty, a fifty-dollar bid, somebody give me fifty, fifty, fifty, yeah! Now fifty-five, fifty-five. Now a hundred. Last chance, does anyone want him for a hundred? Yeah! One hundred! Does anybody want him for one twenty-five? One twenty-five! Yeah! I got one twenty-five over there. Lookin' for a hundred and fifty...one seventy-five. Now *two* hundred...two, two, two. Yeah! Does anybody want him for two and a quarter? Sold him right down here for two hundred dollars."

"Okay. Chute number three...watch this guy for a wild and woolly ride, ladies and gentlemen!"

Bolting out of the chute on the back of a 1,500-pound horse, Meeks races twenty yards into the arena, his hat blowing off his head. Suddenly the horse jerks to a halt, lowers his head, and starts to buck. Meeks moves with the horse, tightening the knuckles of his right hand around the reins while he raises his left arm in the air.

The announcer encourages him to stay on. "Ride 'em, cowboy! Stay with 'im! Hang 'im high!" *(Hoots and hollers)*

Meeks grits his teeth and stays on, matching every move for a full eight seconds. Then a horn blares, and Dale, the pickup man, gallops in. Meeks wraps his arms around Dale's waist and pulls himself from one horse's back to another. The crowd cheers. As soon as he's out of the gate, it's over.

Rodeo people refer to the saddle bronc riding event as the one that shows the process of turning a bronc into a partner. The very symbol of the rodeo is the

# A Cowboy's Prayer

Oh Lord. I've never lived where churches grow
I've loved creation better as it stood
That day you finished it so long ago
And looked upon your work and called it good

Just let me live my life as I've begun
And give me work that's open to the sky
Make me a partner of the wind and sun
And I won't ask for a life that's soft and high

Make me as big and open as the Plains
As honest as the horse between my knees
Clean as the wind that blows behind the rains
Free as the hawk that circles the breeze

Just keep an eye on all that's done and said
Just write me sometime when I turn aside
And guide me on that long, dim travel ahead
That stretches up toward the great divide.

—Badger Clark

Rodeo participants show respect during the reading of A Cowboy's Prayer.

spirited bucking bronco. The image has almost come to stand for the West itself. Riding a bucking horse seems to express the rider's need to connect with the wildness of nature. The power, energy, and strength of the horse uniquely express this elemental force. Anyone who has experience with horses has seen this explosive energy. A well-broke trail horse plodding down a path may suddenly go ballistic if a white plastic sack blows across his path.

Watching Dale Vocu, a talented pickup man, is a sport in itself. The purpose of the pickup man and his horse at a rodeo is to rescue the bucking-bronc rider as

Riding a bucking horse seems to express the rider's need to connect with the wildness of nature.

he is bucked off his horse. Sometimes, the bronc is bucking so hard and fast that a rider can fly off and receive a fatal kick.

There are usually two pairs of pickup men and their horses: One man literally picks up the rider and carries him off on his own horse, while the other rider lures away the runaway bronc. The pickup men and their horses are like cops and their partners cruising in patrol cars. Not only must the pickup men be fearless, willing, and dependable, but so should their horses, since they run alongside the wild broncs. They also should be agile enough to avoid the hooves of the broncs, but at the same time stay near enough to catch the rider as he falls.

When a rider is bucked off his horse a pickup man rescues him.

From April through October, Dale makes his living as a rodeo pickup man—a job that you have to be able to do in less than eight seconds or you could cost a man his life. There are stockmen who would prefer that Dale use his skills to tend to their horses and cattle, dispensing with rodeo life altogether, because they're afraid of losing him. Dale's comely wife, Mona, worries about him every time he goes to work. But Dale Vocu is a popular name among bronc riders. In 1997 he was named Pickup Man of the Year because he can read bucking horses better than anyone. To get to that level, Dale had to experience his share of bucks in the saddle. Decorating his living room are photos of him taken as a saddle bronc rider, along with photos of his two sons doing movie stunt work. Dale has four pickup horses, all of whom he has broken and trained himself. His horses are ready for the rodeo arena by the time they are four or five. Blaze, a sorrel quarter horse, is the fastest.

Just before a rodeo starts, Dale learns which horses are going to be entered in the saddle bronc and bareback riding events. That way he knows if he is getting a reputed kicker or a novice, and he can prepare himself. Sometimes a novice horse is more dangerous because the crowd noise or the arena lights can spook him.

Now it's time for Dale to show us his stuff at the annual Oglala Lakota Nation Powwow and Rodeo. The bucking horse sounds as if he's going to break down the gate. Dale, outfitted in leather-fringed chaps—each leg weighing ten pounds—plus padded skin guards and a protective vest, is mounted, ready, and waiting in the arena. When the horse first comes out of the chute, Dale stays in the shadows for a second or two. A bronc's first and natural tendency always is to go over to the pickup horse, so the pickup man must stay hidden to allow the bronc to perform.

Dale has never had an accident. Keep it up, Dale.

## Postscript —

The rodeo is a legacy originated by the trail and range cowboy, kept alive by modern cowboys and cattlemen of the ranching population. Rodeo is a particularly important part of the traditional way of life for people in the Great Plains, where there is historical continuity between ranching and the cowboy sport.

The Lakota have borrowed these activities from white society because of the convenience, close proximity, and monetary rewards that come from the Indian Rodeo Association, the Indian National Rodeo Finals, and the Professional Rodeo Association. In most events, horses become the riders' helpers.

Dale shows his stuff at the annual Oglala Lakota Nation Powwow and Rodeo.

Rodeo, just like tennis or boxing, is a sport between two opponents, but the opponents are not equally matched. Keep in mind the difference in weight between horse and rider: most rodeo riders weigh an average of 150 pounds; a rodeo horse weighs at least 1,200 pounds. Consider the injuries that rodeo riders can sustain opposed to the horses, who are rarely hurt.

I used to think rodeo was a cruel and brutal sport. But I've changed my opinion after watching some. I know how well-cared-for rodeo horses are. Just like racehorses, rodeo horses are a source of income and for that reason they get the best feed and medical attention possible. And just as Thoroughbreds love to run, so do bucking horses love to buck. (For that matter, most horses buck every once in awhile. Have you ever watched a horse who's been cooped up in bad weather and then is released on a sunny day?) Bucking horses are bred to buck, and consequently have a lot of power.

Dale takes pride in his pickup horse and in his job as a pickup man, which involves keeping both bucking horse and rider safe. It gives him pride in himself and gives him the confidence that comes from controlling and flowing with the power of nature, in this case the bronc. When I was thrown by Moonshadow, I had no one like Dale to rescue me or protect me. I've had to pick myself up in order to ride again. Just as Dale changes from bronc rider to pickup man, I move from the wildness of Moonshadow to my calmer, smaller horse. Learning to ride again with Mollie restores my confidence and gives me a sense of mastery. I'm a more stable person now than I was before my accident.

Dale takes pride in keeping both bucking horse and rider safe.

## Emma and Shelly Waters

Emma Waters is like a mother to me. I met her on my second trip to South Dakota, and almost a year goes by before I visit again. She moved into a new trailer a short way up the hill from her log house and has a postcard view of rolling, pine-dotted hills and a sparkling white church. There is not another house in sight. You can hear a car coming from miles away. After we are reunited and hug each other in her front yard, she says, "You're late!" and "Why don't you write?" She looks vibrant in a turquoise blouse, flowered skirt, and gold necklace. Her hair is permed.

Contrary to popular belief, and despite its history of chiefs and other powerful male figures, the Lakota society is fundamentally matriarchal. Because of this, Emma's role as head of the household comes naturally. Her sons and adopted daughter live in the old log house. The wiry guitar sounds of Jimi Hendrix come wafting out the back window. Emma's kids come outside to greet me, too, along with Little Pauly, a beautiful seven-year-old boy whom I remember from my last visit. I blow up an orange punching balloon for him to play with, but it lasts all of five minutes before a hole deflates it. There are five dogs lounging in the yard, all with varying degrees of mange. I'm warned, "Don't touch them!" only after I've already petted one with a gold earring dangling from his shaggy fur. I wipe my hand on the grass.

Emma retrieves water from a well. She tells one of the boys to make Kool-Aid for us to drink while we sit and talk under the squaw cooler—a politically incorrect name for a shelter of pine limbs covered with boughs. Little Pauly lingers nearby, curious about me.

Shelly, fifteen and gorgeous, tries to catch her white horse, Raccoon, between the garden and the clothesline. Now sixteen years old, Raccoon was broke at four months. His Indian name is *Kiyan Mahi*, which roughly translates to "Flying While Walking." Whenever he hears the beat of a drum, he picks up his hooves and prances. Shelly has ridden Raccoon on the Battle of Little Bighorn Memorial Ride.

Raccoon fills Shelly's heart with joy.

The Battle of Little Bighorn in 1876 is the Lakota's one moment of tremendous victory and celebration. The anger leading up the battle was justified: the buffalo were gradually being killed and the land that had been promised to the Lakota in the 1851 and 1868 Fort Laramie treaties was being flooded with land-hungry settlers, cattlemen, and gold miners.

The story of the battle starts when hundreds of disgruntled Indians fled the reservations to join their brethren in eastern Wyoming and southeastern Montana, and the War Department ordered them back to the Great Sioux Reservation, in

Horses have been crucial to the Lakota's survival for hundreds of years.

western Dakota. Under the wise and powerful leadership of Sitting Bull, no one budged. Then, the 7th Cavalry moved in from the south.

When Lieutenant Colonel George Armstrong Custer arrived in the valley of the Little Big Horn Mountains with the 7th Cavalry, he discovered a village of Indians that included three hundred braves and their horses. With war whoops and explosions from their black-powder firearms, braves plunged into battle on sorrel, bay, and pinto horses, galloping with their heads up and ears forward against a background of blue Montana sky. It was the battle that made Oglala Lakota Crazy Horse famous. He led his braves on a flanking maneuver against Custer that decimated the battalion's right wing and pinned Custer on the low hill, where he made his last stand.

Credit must be given to the horses of the Sioux, for without them there would have been no victory. But the federal government, humiliated by this defeat and fueled by public outrage, retaliated with such vengeance that it put an end to the free-roaming Indian horsemen of North America.

Today, the Black Hills are in the firm grip of the United States. The four presidential faces carved into the rock of Mount Rushmore imply a stolen ownership. To counter Mount Rushmore, the Crazy Horse Memorial, a colossal statue of Crazy Horse mounted on a horse, is being built just 17 miles away. When it's finished, the four faces on Mount Rushmore will fit inside Crazy Horse's head. The horse's head alone is 22 stories high. Crazy Horse's left hand is pointing in answer to a white man's question, "Where are your lands now?" The monument seems to reply, "My lands are where my dead lie buried."

Every year on June 25, which is the anniversary of the Battle of Little Bighorn, a memorial ride begins near the battlefield in the Powder River country of southeastern Montana. The ride helps the Lakota—a small minority group—feel as powerful as the white majority is today. And because the horse was important to the Lakota at the Battle of Little Bighorn, they use the animal today as therapy to recreate the feeling of victory.

The ride is for Indians only, and it cannot be photographed or videotaped. Each day begins with the men doing an early morning charge. On the first day, the riders journey 30 miles; twenty on the second; fifteen on the third; and on the last day, 5 miles. In the lead are six riders, one of whom carries the staff, which resembles a shepherd's staff with eagle feathers hanging from its hook. The staff is a representation of the event itself. The eagle feathers signify honor, integrity, and the code of conduct. Sometimes horse or buffalo hair or deer tail are attached, which are a tribute to the animal. The staff is usually made of cherry or ash wood because both are pliable and hold their shape

Emma grew up on the land that was allotted to her great-grandmother.

once dry. The staff is a sacred object that has to be treated like a newborn baby. It should never hit the ground, nor can riders pass the rider who is carrying the staff.

When the Lakota Sioux signed the 1851 Fort Laramie Treaty, Emma's great-grandmother, *Ta Cank'u win*, or Her Road, was allotted a section, or 640 acres, of land. Emma grew up on this parcel of land, living with her extended family of grandparents, parents, aunts, uncles, and cousins. The wisdom of the grandparents was listened to and life was guided by this wisdom. There was always enough food for them to eat from subsistence farming, but there weren't enough halters and bridles for all the kids to use on the horses. The boys got first dibs, so the girls had to improvise by making bits and reins out of their woolen stockings.

From sunup to sundown, the kids did their chores. Emma remembers having to ride out to the pastures to round up the cattle in winter. Sometimes, white ranchers living nearby took playful shots at her. She says that the whites called them savage dogs and said they should fend for themselves like stray dogs.

"Wendy sits there listening to me talk and laugh and bark," Emma says. She gets up to build a fire, over which she's going to cook the evening meal. I can't imagine the prejudice and hardship that Emma has encountered in her life. She thinks that living on earth has been like being in hell, and she looks forward to the day when she goes to heaven.

## Postscript —

Emma says horses know they're related to Indians, and they can distinguish Indians from other people. Even though she no longer rides, she continues to keep horses because it's the Lakota way of life. It also maintains a connection to the past—not to the days of her youth when she rode her grandfather's ranch land, but before that when land was divided into ranches and government land, back when it couldn't be bought and sold. She keeps horses for her grandchildren so they won't forget their history.

I think of Shelly and Raccoon and all the other horses and riders on the Battle of the Little Bighorn Ride. Not only are they commemorating the battle, but they are putting themselves through the hardship of the long ride to experience as best they can the preparation for battle, the hardship of fighting, and the state of mind necessary to endure the fighting.

On my road to recovery, which feels like a battle every day, I listen to and sing certain songs that give me courage and strength. One such song is "You Gotta Be" by Des'ree. The chorus, "You gotta be hard, you gotta be tough, you gotta be stronger," gets me through many a day.

After meeting Emma and the other Lakota horsepeople, horses take on a new meaning for me. Now when I ride, I often feel that I am participating in Lakota history, its hardships, and resurrection through horses. When I'm in this state of mind, riding gives me a concrete, immediate empathy with the Lakota's struggle for survival. And it makes me feel like a survivor too.

# Wilmer Mesteth

Wilmer Mesteth's grandfather was a chief in Kyle, South Dakota, which is part of the Pine Ridge Reservation. In the 1920s, the chief gave a horse to his son, Elk Eagle, who named him Little White. Elk Eagle and Little White raced at the Stock Growers Association in Crow Agency, Montana, and against the horses of cattlemen in Omaha. Elk Eagle used to ride in chaps and a beaded vest emblazoned with the word, *Rodeo*. Before the races, he sang this special song for himself and Little White.

> Around the world the race horses are gathering
> The horse's name is Little White
> Little White is running first
> And the rest are following behind.
> Eagle Elk, take courage.
> This is your racehorse running first.

When Wilmer was a boy, he and his siblings divided the ownership of the family horses by color: Wilmer had the sorrels; his sister had the buckskins; and his brother, the paints and Appaloosas. Twenty-five years later, Wilmer sold his horses to rodeo legend Howard Hunter Sr., who won four saddle bronc riding championships with them. A quiet man, Wilmer expresses his love for horses in his music and his art.

Lakota songs about horses—of which there are about twenty—are sacred; they can be traced back to the mid-1700s, when horses first appeared on the Great Plains. One characteristic of these songs is brevity. Like haiku, they are composed to extract the greatest possible connotative and denotative meaning from each word. One old Sioux, when asked why the songs are so short, replied: "The songs are short because we know a lot." This wasn't said in the spirit of humor or conceit; instead, it is a statement of fact. Since so many circumstances of a song's composition are already known by the listeners, it is redundant to repeat the details. Songs are also short to dramatize each point by compressing its meaning.

This song is sung each year before the Big Foot Memorial Ride:

*Oyatepi ki blihic'iyapoyo. Si Tanka k'un tehia gliyunkelo.*
*Takini ki heya keya pelo.*

"The people take courage. Big Foot had a hard death.
The survivors are saying this."

—Wilmer Mesteth, 1988

---

The Big Foot Memorial Ride commemorates the Wounded Knee massacre of December 1890. After Sitting Bull was assassinated on December 15, about a hundred of his people joined Chief Si Tanka (Big Foot) and his group of Minneconjou to travel to Pine Ridge, where they hoped to find shelter and protection from the U.S. Cavalry. Unbeknownst to the chief, however, the War Department had just issued a warrant for his arrest and imprisonment, deeming him a "fomenter of distur-

bances." While en route to Pine Ridge, Big Foot contracted pneumonia and had to continue the journey lying in the bed of a wagon. As soon as his band encountered the 7th Cavalry, they raised a white flag in surrender.

The cavalry had plans to hold the Indians at Little Wound Creek until they could escort them to the Union Pacific Railroad for transport to a military prison in Omaha. In the meantime, the soldiers trained a battery of big Hotchkiss guns on them. The next morning, the soldiers gathered the Indian men together and demanded all of their weapons. During this interaction, there was a misunderstanding between some troopers and a young brave who was deaf. A skirmish followed and shots rang out. Since few of the Indians were armed, they began to run. That's when the guns on the hill opened fire and slaughtered more than 250 men, women, and children as though they were a herd of buffalo. Since a snowstorm was starting, many of the dead were left where they had fallen. Big Foot's frozen corpse was half-raised, as if he were trying to get up. Eventually, it was thrown in a mass grave with 140 other corpses.

The idea for the ride came to a descendant of a massacre survivor during a recurring dream. The riders retrace the 300-mile trail of Chief Big Foot and his band, which includes sliding down the sheer, ice-covered cliffs of the Badlands on horseback. The riders trot single file, heads held high. One year on the ride, the temperature was 42 below with zero visibility; another time, black-and-white photos were taken of the riders approaching the massacre site, and ghostlike images of Indians wrapped in blankets mysteriously appeared in the foreground of the pictures.

The horse was important at the time Chief Big Foot and his followers returned to Pine Ridge. Today, the Big Foot memorial Ride participants show that the Lakota are resilient and everlasting, and that the horse is still a symbol of life

The Wounded Knee cemetery is a landmark for all to see.

for their society. Whether one is directly or indirectly involved in the Big Foot Memorial Ride, the event helps people come to terms with loss and grief.

The Lakota have ceremonies that honor their horses. Some are private; only members of the tribe are allowed to attend. Typical of these are the ceremonies of the Horse Medicine societies, which are attended by a horse medicine man, who is credited with healing powers that he obtained in a dream or vision. Using these powers, he can heal sick people as well as influence the weather. In such a rite, praying, singing, drumming, and dancing occurs with sacred paraphernalia such as horse effigies or wooden dance sticks (like the one I purchased at Windspirit Gallery).

# My Horse

my horse
flying
along
I have caused
a medicine
to wear
I caused my own
flying
along
I have caused

— "My Horse," sung by Lone Man

---

In the early days, dance sticks were carved of specific horses who had been killed in battle; this kept their memory alive. They were used for power in horse raids and battle. The carving was painted with colors extracted from clays and fruit juices, and they were decorated with rawhide ears and a bridle. The

A slain medicine man at Wounded Knee.

The dead are carted away to a mass grave.

mane and tail were made from the dead horse's mane and tail. The fatal wounds also were etched into the wood and stained red. Today, horse dance sticks can be found at powwows, galleries, and museums. As part of his artwork, Wilmer carves a variety of dance sticks.

## Postscript —

Although Wilmer currently doesn't own horses, he maintains a strong spiritual connection to them through his songs and sculptures. It is a healthy substitute.

While I was recovering from my accident—before I could ride and particularly when I was using a walker, crutches, or cane—I often wore heavy silver rings or bracelets with carvings of horses to make me feel physically and emotionally strong and to convey to others that I wasn't weak. Today, even though my arm and legs have healed, I feel a secret inward pleasure and sense of security when I wear clothing designed with horse figures or when I wear Elizabeth Arden's Blue Grass perfume, which is contained in a bottle bearing an emblem of a horse. I am certain this feeling is similar to that which Lakota horsepeople experience.

Dance sticks were carved of specific horses to keep their memory alive.

# Reservation Cowboy

I'm a reservation cowboy
And the Badlands is where
I make my home
I ride upon a saddle
And this here horse
Is all I own.

I once had me a cowgirl
And Lord, she loved the things we did
But she met a city slicker
And I guess that's all that should be said.

But you know I sometimes kinda' miss her
'Specially when the moon is shining bright
And when the coyotes are howling
I ride all alone in the night.

Now if you're ever feeling lonely
And the whole world seems to get you down
Well, pack your things, my partner
And leave that smoggy old town.

And you can be a reservation cowboy
And call the Badlands your home
And you can ride upon a saddle
And have a horse all your own
'Cuz I'm a reservation cowboy.

—Buddy Red Bow

# Vernell White Thunder

"Bring chocolate," Vernell White Thunder says and hangs up the phone. So I stop at Big Bat's convenience store in Pine Ridge and buy a bag of Hershey's bars. This is a welcome departure from the packs of cigarettes I'm usually asked to bring as gifts to the Lakota I visit. (Even though Indians think tobacco is sacred, I don't want to cause anyone to get lung cancer.) So with everything in the car, I set out to meet Vernell, the horseman everyone knows on the Pine Ridge Reservation.

Driving down the Bureau of Indian Affairs Route 2, I pass fields of dry sunflowers, their blackish brown faces turned in the same direction, and miles of rolling pea-green hills that look as if they've been dusted with corn flour. You'd think a ranch outside the small town of Kyle, population 914, wouldn't be hard to find. Think again. There are no street signs, or house numbers. Instead, Vernell's directions are: "Make a right sometime after the bridge...after the store go left...drive a couple of miles..."

To Vernell, the most distinguishing feature of his place are the seven white-walled rubber tires out front. As I drive, I find out that just about everybody has tires out front. I pass Vernell's house at least twice. Finally, I count the tires and realize they are *the* rubber tires I'm told to look for. I turn down the long dirt driveway.

At first, it seems as if no one is home. A sorrel-and-white stallion with an injured front foot is grazing in the front yard, which appears to have been just mowed. The horse looks as if he has been in someone's good care for a long time. I knock on the door to the screened-in front porch, but there is no answer. I cup my

Gleefully, Vernell gallops after his horses.

hands around my eyes and peer inside. Saddles and bridles hang from racks and hooks, but there is nobody inside. I walk around to the back of the house. Pink snapdragons and white daisies are planted along the side. Still, there is no sign of anyone. Beyond the driveway is a bright blue corral instead of the usual metal kind. But there isn't a single horse inside. Have I turned up the wrong driveway?

Suddenly, I feel the ground under my feet vibrate, and I hear the sound of stampeding hooves. I spin around to see a herd of black-and-white paints racing in from the back field. At first, I think the horses are wild and I want to run as they head toward me,

A herd of black-and-white paints race in from the pasture.

but then, rounding the bend is a man on horseback whooping, "AAAIIIEEEYA!"

Vernell looks like every woman's dream of an Indian horseman. His light blue denim shirt with cut-off sleeves reveals smooth, muscular arms. A black ponytail glints in the rays of the sun. High atop his horse, he is in control of his herd of paints as he maneuvers them into the corral. Yet he appears wild and impulsive as he spins his horse around and keeps the flashy paints moving in a fast, tight circle. Then he makes them change direction. After this performance, Vernell casually dismounts. He takes off his hat and shyly approaches me.

With pride, Vernell White Thunder tells me that he owns seventy-two horses— many of them paints—which he keeps on his 1,100 acres. He had inherited the land from his grandfather. It's not an unusually large amount of land for one to have on the reservation, considering Pine Ridge consists of more than 1 million acres. When his grandfather first came to the U.S. from Canada, he brought a herd of two hundred.

For ten years, Vernell was an employee of the federal government. Then he taught school for another ten years. But he wasn't happy until he was around horses—like when he was a boy, helping his grandfather. According to Vernell, the horse has a soul. The soul of the horse absorbs what we're feeling. If you're angry or tense, you shouldn't ride; do something else or just walk outside and spend time with your horse. When you're feeling patient and calm, that's the time to ride because a horse requires you to know and understand his limitations. "Long ago Indians and horses were related. We thought of our horses as grandsons."

Vernell had come riding in on his best round-up horse, a brown-and-white paint named Windwalker. The grass-nibbling stud in the front yard is War Paint—a horse Vernell traded five horses for because he had "something in him. Even if he was a little bit dingy in the head." "Indian horses have always been the fastest and strongest—even when they look half-starved—because they have a strong constitution from feeding on tree bark and brush." In fact, Vernell tells me that his father, Guy White Thunder, used to doctor a sick horse by tying a bag of burning cedar embers around the horse's snout to inhale. Then he would sing him a sacred song.

Vernell breeds his stock for color, conformation, and disposition; and his horses are in big demand, he says. He sells to the rich and famous back East; the Bass family of Texas is a client. In Vernell's bureau drawers are photos of him with Ted Turner and Jane Fonda. He has a special Stetson, still in its original paisley hatbox, from the late Mary Kay of Mary Kay Cosmetics. He frequently sells his horses to people in Spain and Switzerland, but he also sells locally to those who will give one of his horses a good home. (He knows his horses go to good homes because he visits the future owners—no matter where they live—to see how many friends they have and how they treat their other pets.) The going price is "anything from a bad check to $10,000," he says with a grin.

Before the day gets too warm, we pile into his pickup truck for a tour of his land. Five miles down the road is a pasture full of mares and their foals. We get out and walk toward them. A few yearlings edge close to their mothers. I'm leery of

Vernell discovers the remains of one of his old horses.

these horses because horses on the reservation have less contact with people than the horses I'm used to. Their behavior is more unpredictable. "Do you size up a horse when you first meet it?" I ask.

"No, you approach a horse with confidence, letting it know that you're not afraid of it and it needn't be afraid of you."

When I get to the middle of the field, I stand quietly and let the horses gather around me. I meet a chestnut mare (as in the Roger McGuinn song) who used to be a bucking horse in the rodeo. I've never thought of mares as bucking horses; she is curious and friendly. As I rub her satin neck, she closes her eyes and leans into the caress of my hand. I fall in love with her gentleness. At the end of our visit, she follows me back to the truck. I want to take her home.

Farther out in the pasture, Vernell finds the sun-bleached skull of one of his old horses. He picks it up carefully and examines it, wondering which of his horses it might have been. Out here on the Plains, the pasture also serves as a graveyard. When a horse lies down for the last time, nobody buries him or picks him up for disposal. Nature takes over as wolf, coyote, or mountain lion eat the flesh off the bones.

We drive to the next pasture, picking wild plums and chokecherries through the open windows. "This is a good time for roundup cuz lunch is provided." Then Vernell gets out of his truck to pick sage and purple bee plant. When he returns, he ties the bouquet to his rearview mirror, telling me it is a natural aromatizer.

Horses are Vernell's life, but he admits he's looking for a woman. He wants someone who doesn't care about the bright lights, make-up, or fancy clothes of the big city, someone who will kiss a baby as easily as she can handle a horse. His horses are his life. Vernell prays that his horses go to good homes and that they will find enough to eat in the winter.

It has been a good day at the White Thunder Ranch, and as a special treat for Vernell, we drive to the Burger King in Rapid City. We take the long route so I can see the Badlands. As we pass through what looks like the ancient remains of a fallen city, the sun is on the horizon, casting shadows in the crevices of rock. Towheaded tourists look as if they are trying to read the rocks like a map.

On the way back from Rapid City, it's pouring rain. I pull the sleeves of my sweatshirt down over my hands. Flashes of lightning outline the craggy peaks of the Badlands. On KILI, 90.1, the disc jockey repeatedly warns against driving drunk. I'm happy when we finally spot Vernell's porch light. He invites me inside to hear him play his guitar.

When I finally head back to Rushville, I drive a deserted two-lane road in utter blackness. In the sweep of my headlights, I see more fields of sunflowers. This

The sweeter side of Vernell White Thunder.

time, their brown heads are all facing me like expectant guests at a surprise party. In this case, the appropriate guest of honor would be Vernell White Thunder—charming with people and at the top of his game.

# Postscript—

In addition to being a symbolic value and emotional benefit, horses have provided Vernell with an income and a way of economically integrating into society. His economic success from breeding and selling horses has elevated his position in the community, which, in turn, has led him to establish a reputation as a representative of the Pine Ridge Reservation. As a representative, he offers lodging and tours on horseback to visitors. Every time I speak to Vernell on the phone, he has people staying with him, and they come from all over the world, especially from Europe. His status has allowed him to reach beyond his own culture and act as an ambassador of sorts to people who want to learn more about the Lakota.

Yet despite his financial success with horses, Vernell maintains a uniquely Lakota spirituality in his thinking about horses and has never become materialistic. As I learn about his beliefs, I become more aware of the similarity between his reality and the way I experience horses. As a working woman, I'm obligated to focus on my economic survival and materialistic needs. This means keeping my skills relevant to employers so I can earn a regular paycheck. Oftentimes, my life feels like drudgery because financial success by itself has never been meaningful enough to fulfill me. However, my relationships with horses have provided a path, enabling me to stay connected to my more vital, fundamental needs.

# Pat Heathershaw

*"There's a fine line between breaking an animal and breaking its spirit."*

Pat Heathershaw is what some people would call a breed or mixed blood. These terms not only indicate his biological inheritance but also his way of life. Pat is more tuned in to the ethos of American culture—of "getting ahead"—than most people living on the reservation. Yet the reservation is his homeland and he identifies himself as Lakota. (Pat's mother was Oglala Lakota and his father was white. His dad worked as a park ranger in the Badlands National Park, which is how he met Pat's mom.)

To get to Pat's ranch, I have to drive 8 miles from the main highway, through Interior, South Dakota, over six cattle guards, and past one Do Not Enter sign. But when I arrive at the ranch, I think I have found heaven. I park in the shade of a big apple tree and get out of the car. Reddish green fruit covers the ground, and four tiny kittens jump off the front porch and scamper over to me.

I walk up to the gray-shingled house and rap on the screen door, but no one seems to be around, despite all the family names listed on a wooden plaque. Then I see Pat's note:

*Wendy,*

*I am about 1½ miles south of the house, driving tractor, or in the*

*hayfield. I'll be back about 6:00 or 7:00 P.M.*

There's a diagram showing me the two locations where I can find him. It's 5:45. I decide to look around.

Chickens, roosters, and ducks meander around the yard. A buffalo, whose eyes remind me of Bette Davis's, shares a corral with two paint stallions. Every time the bison turns toward the fowl, they scatter because he has quite a presence; his inhaling and exhaling sound as if they come from a place deep inside of him.

In the yard on a white wooden table with red wheels, sits a coffee kettle and two cast-iron skillets. A long, skinny brook where the kittens drink their water slices its way across the property and provides a soothing sound. The kittens—one charcoal, one calico, and the other two mixed—are now somersaulting in a haystack. Perpendicular between two trees is an extralong hitching post made from two tree limbs. The skull of an old steer hangs over the barn door. A lot of branding irons, each with a different design, hang next to the door. Most ranchers use just one branding-iron design to distinguish their livestock, but Pat has an entire collection.

Inside the barn, the smell of hay, old leather tack, and wood take me back to my childhood days of visiting family friends on their farms. From the westward window, particles of dust dance in the shaft of evening sunlight. And the constant buzzing of flies puts me in a peaceful trance. To kill time, I inspect the different bits, from snaffle to grazing, that hang from pegs on the wall.

A welcoming sight on Pat's front porch.

At 7:30 P.M., Pat drives in from the field on his tractor. A yellow dog much like Old Yeller runs alongside him. Pat gets off the tractor and approaches cautiously. He has a stern look about him. When I tell him how much I like his place, a big grin stretches across his face. He is handsome, sort of a cross between Paul Newman and Henry Fonda.

Pat keeps about thirty head of buffalo and sells the calves. He has more than one hundred horses. The mares and colts are kept the farthest away in the biggest pasture, which is in the Badlands. The colts get strong from a lot of exercise and stretching, and their hooves get tough from the rocky soil. In the winters, Pat has watched his horses take turns pawing through the ice to get at the grass; the horse with the strongest hooves breaks the ice for the others.

The buffalo in the corral had been broke to ride as a yearling, then was not ridden for a while. Pat bought him recently, intending to break him all over again. He works with him just as he would a horse—in a round pen with a rope. He gets

With great care, Pat trains his buffalo to be ridden like a horse.

the buffalo trotting, then loping around the arena. Then Pat stops him with a "Whoa," walks right up to him, and strokes his fuzzy head.

"There's a fine line between breaking an animal and breaking its spirit," he turns to me and says.

Looking at this immense creature and trying to imagine Pat riding him, I can't help but think of the impressions of William Darnell, an early settler.

*...Our wagon train had been traveling homeward in the usual monotonous manner, when suddenly the driver in the lead wagon yelled back the words, "Buffalo! Buffalo! Buffalo!" A big herd was coming into sight, and the wagon train was in the direct path of the animals, and buffaloes rarely turned aside for anything. The members of the wagon train were in a perilous position, as well as their teams. Whatever was to be done had to be done quickly. At once an order went forth, "Close up the train in the form of a wedge." This was done with all possible dispatch, and forty dragoons who accompanied the train as a protection against Indians were stationed at the point of the wagon train, forming a compact triangle where the buffalo would meet.*

*On came those galloping, shaggy monsters. The whole landscape seemed to be one vast dark-brown flood, which rose and fell with the contour of the ground, stretching out on either side as far as the eye could reach, and extending away to the north where the end was lost to sight. There were thousands upon thousands, more likely millions, of them in that herd.*

*Scarcely had the men got the wagons in position with the dragoons in front than the herd approached like one vast floor, the sound of their hoofs striking the earth resembling the roll of thunder. When about twenty-five yards distant, the dragoons fired point blank into the vanguard, hoping this would divide the herd. Everyone in the train held his breath awaiting the outcome, fearing his last hour had come. At a point but a few feet from the dragoons the herd divided, galloping by and uniting once more when the last wagon had been passed, surrounding the wagon train, much like an island in the middle of a turbulent sea. On they came like an overwhelming flood, the whole landscape as far as the eye could reach in every direction being one seething mass, and moving southward. It was a sight one sees but once in a lifetime, and under conditions one would not care to repeat. How slowly the time seemed to drag as they went charging by. After an eternity we could see the herd's proportions were beginning to diminish, and finally when the few last stragglers galloped by one of the crowd who had glanced at this watch at the start, remarked that a little more than a half hour had elapsed from the time the herd reached them and had gone by*

*The only casualty to our outfit happened to one of the horses, which in some unaccountable manner had a knee shot off.*

Charging buffalo are so overwhelming that it's amazing the Lakota had the nerve to ride alongside or into these herds. But that is why many a Lakota considered his buffalo horse to be his most dependable friend—much of the success in procuring food for the tribe was based on how well the two worked together. As soon as the horse heard the twang of the bowstring, a good buffalo horse swerved away from his victim to get out of harm's way before the wounded animal turned and charged.

Today, rodeo riding is the closest one can come to showcasing the skill and daredevil riding of the old days. With that in mind, Pat created the Oglala-Lakota Nonprofit Tipi Camp and Rodeo School at his ranch in the Badlands. It's free to cardholding members of the South Dakota High School Rodeo Association and accommodates 35 students for instruction in bareback, saddle bronc, and bull riding. The boys camp out in authentic Lakota tepees and eat chuck wagon cooking, including buffalo meat. Those who receive "Best in the Event" receive a handmade bronc saddle and protective vest. The Oglala Lakota Tribal Council donates the funding, South Dakota rodeo producers donate the bucking bulls, and Dr. Skip

Ross and his sports medicine team are on hand in case there are any injuries.

Pat says he wants to help kids because many people helped him in his youth. He also feels that tomorrow's leaders in South Dakota will come from ranches owned for hundreds of years by the same family, just like the one he grew up on. He says, "We may well have a future tribal president and a South Dakota governor who both attended my school. If, twenty years from now, the tribal president and the governor are good friends because they met and became acquainted at this camp, then I will be a very proud man."

At the camp, the kids experience a taste of their forefathers' life, whether they were Indians or cowboys. They get to touch the pulse of the great horse culture of the Plains, interact at a grassroots level with untamed horses, and traverse old pathways for their strength and wisdom.

In the old days, the kids of Pine Ridge rode through town on horseback. Fewer and fewer kids today own horses. Pat asks me the question, "Will our humanity [toward one another] ever surpass our technology? This camp focuses on humanity and on getting back to basics and giving kids something to be proud of. For those who live in town, it will be their first experience living on the land."

## Postscript—

Pat is strengthened by teaching others the horsemanship skills required for rodeo. Teaching is a way for him to share his own joy in riding. I frequently derive a similar pleasure when I have an opportunity to introduce a child to horses and riding. Recently a friend asked if she could bring her grandson to meet Mollie. At four years, he already loves horses. His favorite movie is *Spirit: Stallion of the Cimarron*, which he has watched over and over. On the day he comes to the ranch, I can see by the expression on his face that he is completely blown away by being in the presence of so many horses. At first he is a little inhibited around Mollie, but after feeding, riding, and helping me bathe her, he does not want to leave until his grand-

mother promises they'll return. By recognizing a child's feelings toward my horse, I'm able to reexperience my own pleasure with her.

I also see much of myself in Pat's desire to challenge modern life by getting back to basics through horses. Whenever I'm in the rural area that surrounds Mollie's ranch, I leave the city behind and feel part of a less technological and more humane time and place. Pat understands that to know a horse well, a rider must be sensitive to what the animal feels. This has a humanizing affect on the rider, which, in turn, makes the rider more sensitive to the feeling of vulnerability and dependence in other people. Adapting this same philosophy has allowed me to be more understanding and less critical of other people

Pat spots his son, guiding the horses home.

## Lester Waters

The old horse society is alive and well in Wayne's brother, Lester. In addition to being a tribal police officer, he keeps eighty horses (all of them paints except for a palomino and a red roan). His horses have beautiful markings such as a white lightning-bolt dash streaking across a horse's black neck. Recently, he added to his herd by purchasing a few wild mustangs from the Bureau of Land Management, and he says they're doing well.

Although he uses only some of his horses, he keeps so many because they give him satisfaction and make him feel proud. The size of a person's herd signifies a type of wealth to the Lakota. Lester intends to train and sell some of his horses as bucking horses, who go for about $10,000 each.

When I first meet Lester, it is a warm, dry day in August. We sit outside on his front porch overlooking the little town of Pine Ridge, surrounded by small homes

# Many Horses Die in Snow Winter

Many horses die for lack of grass.
Unable to eat snow
unable to paw through it,
they are given away to Winter
as if they never had an owner.

—Gerald Hausman

Lester's beguiling horses have unusual markings.

with flower gardens and manicured green lawns. On the hill in the distance is an early twentieth century, faintly ominous-looking building that once served as a hospital.

Lester's father, Bud Waters, and a horsewoman named Lois White Whirlwind are also at the house. As we converse, people in their pickup trucks stop by to chat. I learn that the western side of the reservation is influenced by the vaqueros who led cattle drives from Texas in the 1800s. Therefore, the Lakota of western Pine Ridge like the look of Spanish-style tack such as silver bits and conches.

Later, we take a ride to the family ranch. From across the highway, Lyle, Lester's eldest, rides a five-year-old black-and-white paint out of the pasture. Like

Lyle rides a five-year-old black-and-white paint out of the pasture.

his father, Lyle breaks and trains horses for others. The quick-stepping gate of the horse conveys gentleness and strength all at the same time. Seeing them come over the hillside lit by the late afternoon sun takes me back two hundred years. As they approach, the horse bows his head and Lyle takes on the aura of a humble warrior.

Lester says that when he has a bad day at the police station, he likes to get into his truck and drive over to the pasture to be with the horses. So we climb into the front seat of his pickup and drive up and over hillsides until we are face-to-face with a herd of paint mares. They stand and stare at us, and we stare back. Their beauty is so phantasmic that I feel as though I'm in another world, yet I can hear their breath and smell their sweat. It isn't until Lester turns the ignition that they take off running. A beautiful sight.

"We had a really bad winter," Lester says. "I lost a lot of horses,"

I turn and see the sadness in his eyes.

"The vet told me that if a pregnant horse's coat isn't warm enough, the horse will absorb the fetus she is carrying for warmth."

As I had promised, I ask Lester about his brother Wayne's horse. Lester is doubtful that we'll be able to track him down. Chief is elusive. No one sees him in the same place twice. We drive across pastures and down dirt roads, visiting all the places in which Chief might be lurking—in a gully, behind a tree, over a hillside. No luck. I know that Wayne will be disappointed, but Lester shrugs his shoulders. A horse is a horse.

Cass, another of Lester's boys, has entered the bucking bronco event at the upcoming rodeo. He says he rides for the thrill—the adrenaline rush. Cass doesn't plan to leave the reservation and compete with the rest of the world; he thinks leaving will bring trouble. He perceives the world around him as hostile and unpredictable so he is convinced he can't achieve success in it. Yet he was willing to spend eight seconds on the back of an animal that can possibly cripple him for life.

# Postscript—

I know exactly how Lester feels when he says that after a bad day at work he likes to unwind by driving over to the pasture and watching his horses. I experience the same relaxation at the ranch where I board Mollie. It's a place where I can escape. The pace of life slows me down. I might have to drive like a woman possessed to get there, but as soon as I walk up to Mollie and start talking to her in a soft, calm voice, I begin to relax. The act of grooming her relaxes me further. Scientific studies have shown that petting a dog or cat lowers one's blood pressure, and I think working with my horse has a similar effect.

As I go about my chores, nature casts her spell with lively songbirds and intoxicating orange poppies, purple lavender, and yellow daisies. My trainer, Glen, asks me what's new before we start a lesson, and I get to talk about anything I like. Sometimes we begin with a trail ride, which helps me release my thoughts and Mollie gets to stretch her legs. On the trail, cactus and mustard plants are blooming and the Tujunga Wash is filled with rainwater.

After I put Mollie in her stall, I like to linger at the door and listen to the rhythmic *chomp, chomp* of her as she munches hay. I am dirty and gritty and my hair is plastered to my scalp, but I don't care. By the time I get back on the freeway to go home, I am so relaxed that I can barely keep the speedometer up to 60 mph.

Lester wonders why I want a horse with a blind eye. To me, she is beautiful, patient, intuitive, and fun. She has been the right horse to help me overcome my fear of riding after suffering such a crippling accident and lengthy recovery.

The burning spirit of a horse at sunset.

# The Carlows

The Carlows are one happy family, the Brady Bunch of Pine Ridge. The youngest, nine-year-old Kayla, is like the little engine that could. About the size of my pinkie finger with long honey-colored hair, she wears cowboy boots with spurs and a baseball cap. When I arrive she gets on her miniature horse and rides around the property as if she's on a motorbike.

Darwin "Bogie" Carlow, a Tribal Council member, takes an active role in youth rodeo. He and his pretty wife, Donna, have three other children besides Kayla: Reena, 17; Monte, 14; and Bogie Junior, 12. Both Bogie Junior and Kayla have won silver buckles in timed events at the rodeo, and Reena has been crowned Miss Indian Rodeo Queen, for which she has a silver crown.

The Carlows have 9,000 acres of pastureland, where they keep cows and horses. Their one stud, Studley, is an overo (predominantly white) paint horse. At first, he is cautious about approaching the family's red truck, but once he decides to come over, we can't get rid of him. He's curious about everything and sneaks up behind me in the field to look over my shoulder.

We can't be sure which is the lead mare; none of them show any dominance in their behavior. Initially, they all approach us with their ears pointed forward. Then they stop about 10 feet away, and if we take a step toward them, they retreat as one. Later, they become bored with us and wander off—all except Studley and a sorrel paint mare.

Back home at their ranch, the family keeps ten horses in a corral. These include two miniatures, Lonnie and Jo-Jo, who the kids purchased with money from rodeo wins. They also have a baby deer, appropriately named Baby, chickens, turkeys, a wild duck, rabbits, cats, and a pack of dogs. There is a goat, too.

About seven years ago, Donna suffered a horseback riding accident. While working a new horse, she was injured when he tried to buck her off, then reared up, and flipped over on his back. The saddle horn punctured her stomach and there was

The Carlow clan is all shapes and sizes.

blood everywhere. Bogie Junior was sick for a week from seeing his mother so badly injured. Donna was whisked to Rapid City (three hours away) in an ambulance, and was in surgery for six hours. The doctors thought they might have to remove her colon, but in the end she got to keep it with the help of a hundred stitches.

Six weeks later, it was time to round-up the animals to a different part of the pasture, and because she didn't want to be left out of this family activity, she planned to be back on a horse for the event. But when was time for her to mount

Thoughtful, Donna prepares to ride.

up, her hands got clammy and her mouth went dry. Even today, when she sees someone fall backward on a horse, she gets the chills.

Donna's motivation to get back to horseback riding isn't just for the family roundup—she decides that she wants to try barrel racing. As a kid, her parents had always discouraged her from the sport because they felt it isn't a constructive thing to do on a horse—it's just for pleasure. Now, she has a barrel-racing horse named Jack, and she belongs to a barrel-racing club that meets every two weeks at a different location. There are about fifteen people in the club, both kids and adults. She has set up a course in her own yard for practice, and she says she has beaten Kayla once.

An award-winning family.

Since my first visit with the Carlows, Bogie Senior has passed away. In the old days, a dead man's favorite horse sometimes was sacrificed so that the close relationship that existed between man and beast might continue in the spirit world. The horse would be decorated with feathers and painted with pictographs showing the owner's coups. Needless to say, this custom is kaput.

Today, the Carlow kids are teenagers and are doing typical teenage things: Bogie Junior and Monte break curfew; Kayla wants to drive the family car; and Reena is engaged to be married. Life goes on for them, and I wish them all the best.

# Postscript—

Riders who have a major horseback riding accident also have a unique opportunity to test themselves and even to be strengthened by the ordeal. I think Donna's Lakota background gave her powerful motivation to overcome her catastrophe; remaining a horsewoman means keeping her precious identity as a Lakota. I've had to struggle with my own riding accident and, like Donna, had to repair my mind after my body was healed. Going through my own riding disaster, recovering the use of my legs, and acclimating to the replacement of my hip has been a transformational phase of my life.

I often wish I'd received more support from my family in particular and society in general while I was getting back to riding. Unlike Donna, I developed my love of riding in a culture that doesn't place as much value on it as does the Lakota's culture. Donna was able to bounce back from her physical and emotional injuries with the nurturing support of Lakota horse culture. My recovery forced me to delve into the resources within myself. When Donna told me her story, I got a sense of comfort and relief from the solitary nature of my own recovery, and it broke through my isolation.

Pop's pride and joy.

# They Will Appear

They will appear—may you behold them!

They will appear—may you behold them!

A horse nation will appear.

A thunder-being nation will appear.

They will appear, behold!

They will appear, behold!

*~In the Trail of the Wind: American Indian Poems and Ritual Orations*

# PART FOUR

# The Future of Lakota Horsepeople

I hope that I have crystallized for you an understanding of the meaning of the horse in Lakota culture and history. I also hope that I have helped some Lakota people rediscover their cultural identity and gain strength to resolve some of their social problems.

The Lakota people have preserved the emotional power of their ancient culture and strength as a people by maintaining their love for horses. Riding horses in the Sobriety, Bigfoot, Crazy Horse, and Little Bighorn rides has reawakened their identity as members of a victorious nation. Their activities as horsepeople in their everyday lives have fostered the core Lakota values of physical courage and bravery.

The sense of nationhood among the Lakota has evolved into a loyalty to the United States and has been manifested by a high rate of volunteerism for military service. In every American war since World War I, a large percentage of American Indians have fought in the armed services. And just as Indian warriors once decorated their horses before battle to give them special powers, the U.S. military, borrowing from Indian cultures, has given its attack aircraft names such as *Tomahawks* and *Kiowas*, thereby presenting an image of speed and accuracy. The United States is fortunate to have the Lakota horsepeople as its allies.

Some Lakota who enlist do so because it gives them an honorable opportunity to leave the reservation without feeling they have abandoned their people. It also allows them to see the rest of the world from a protected vantage point. Sadly, it is sometimes safer to be an Indian in the military than it is to be an Indian off the reservation. Wayne's nephew Cass already is afraid of leaving the reservation because he thinks he won't be able to make it in the unfamiliar and potentially hostile world outside.

California, especially Los Angeles where many American Indians work as actors and musicians, is one of the few states where discrimination against Indians is minimal. It is not hard to understand why 10 percent of the native population in the United States lives in the Golden State. If we can put aside our prejudices and welcome the contributions that American Indians make, then our nation will be that much more culturally enriched.

One of the qualities of the Lakota is their connection to the animal world. As the pressures of modern life pull me away from feeling part of nature, it is therapeutic for me to connect with a culture more integrated with animals. This connection helps me remember who I really am. It is knowledge more profound than knowledge simply based on knowing facts about one's self. This is revealed to me when my everyday identity is stripped away by an experience so intense and genuine that I remain forever changed. I have discovered that when I allow myself to enter the intuitive world of the Oglala Lakota and their horses, I am transformed.

While I was interviewing the Lakota people, I not only felt a part of their community, but I also began to strongly identify with the individuals. Each one has taught me a lesson: Moon Weston and Donna Carlow, who both had serious accidents, successfully reestablished a bond with horses; Lester Waters surrounds himself with horses in a natural environment to deal with stress; Vernell White Thunder and Emma Waters uphold the belief that horses are their kin; Dale Vocu partners with horses to achieve an athletic goal; Eugenio White Hawk, Pat Heathershaw, Wendell Yellow Bull, as well as Billy and Phillip Jumping Eagle work with horses to help their community; Aldean Twiss realizes that horses can help one find a path in life that isn't self-destructive; Wilmer Mesteth transfers his feeling about horses to art; and Wayne Waters—no matter where life leads him—believes that horses can take him to a place in his heart called home.

Ever since the Lakota people taught me the healing power of horses, my own experience of riding has become more therapeutic and meaningful. I feel more connected to my horse, Mollie, and that connection makes me feel close to the Lakota people. As both horsepeople and nonriders alike read the interviews that comprise this book, I hope that they will also identify with these struggling, yet heroic people, and appreciate the healing power of horses in their lives.

The collected strength of a herd of Lakota horses.

# Bibliography

American Indian Relief Council. Rapid City, S.D., 1999. http://www.airc.org/html.

Black Elk, Henry, Blue Thunder, Kate, Clairmont, Irene, and Dunham, Christine. *Buckskin Tokens: Contemporary Oral Narratives of the Lakota.* Aberdeen, SD: North Plains Press, 1975.

Calloway, Colin G., Ed. *Our Hearts Fell to the Ground: Plains Indians Views of How the West Was Lost.* New York: St. Martin's, 1996.

Capps, Benjamin. *The Old West: The Indians.* New York: Time-Life Books, 1973.

Cohen, Bill, Ed. *Stories and Images About What the Horse Has Done for Us.* Pentiction, British Columbia, Theytus Books, Ltd., 1998.

Denhardt, Robert Moorman. *The Horse of the Americas.* Norman, OK: University of Oklahoma, 1947.

Densmore, Frances. *Teton Sioux Music.* Washington, D.C.: Smithsonian Institution, Bureau of American Ethnology, Government Printing Office, 1918.

Donnelly, Ernest John. *The History and Romance of the Horse.* New York: Dover Publications, 1946.

Griffith, T.D. *South Dakota.* Oakland, CA: Compass American Guides, 1998.

Hassrick, Royal B. *The Sioux: Life and Customs of a Warrior Society.* Norman, OK: University of Oklahoma Press, 1964.

Hausman, Gerald. *Meditations with Animals: A Native American Bestiary.* Santa Fe, NM: Bear & Company, 1986.

Hoxie, Frederick, Ed. *Encyclopedia of North American Indians.* New York: Houghton Mifflin Company, 1996.

Irwin, Chris. *Horses Don't Lie: What Horses Teach Us About Our Natural Capacity for Awareness, Confidence, Courage, and Trust.* New York: Marlowe & Company, 2001.

Iverson, Peter. *When Indians Became Cowboys: Native Peoples and Cattle Ranching in the American West.* Norman, OK: University of Oklahoma Press, 1994.

Lawrence, Elizabeth Atwood. *Hoofbeats and Society: Studies of Human-Horse Interactions.* Bloomington, IN: Indiana University Press, 1985.

Lawrence, Elden Eugene. "Returning to Traditional Beliefs and Practices: A Solution for Indian Alcoholism." *Dissertation Abstracts International: The Humanities and Social Sciences* 60, no. 12 (June 2000).

Lowe, Robert H. *Indians of the Plains.* Garden City, New York: The American Museum of Natural History, 1954.

McCormick, Adele von Rüst, PhD, and McCormick, Marlena Deborah, PhD *Horse Sense and the Human Heart: What Horses Can Teach Us About Trust, Bonding, Creativity, and Spirituality.* Deerfield Beach, Florida: Health Communications, Inc., 1997.

McGinnis, Anthony. *Counting Coup and Cutting Horses: Intertribal Warfare on the Northern Plains 1738-1889.* Evergreen, CO: Cordillera Press, 1990.

McGuane, Thomas. *Some Horses.* New York: The Lyons Press, 1999.

Mails, Thomas E. *The Mystic Warriors of the Plains.* Garden City, New York: Doubleday & Company, Inc., 1972.

_____. *Plains Indians: Dog Soldiers, Bear Men and Buffalo Women.* New York: Bonanza Books, 1973.

Melmer, David. "Rodeo Riders Compete for the Gold." *Indian Country Today,* January 23, 2002.

_____. "Whiteclay Urged to Clean Up Its Image," *Indian Country Today,* June 23, 2003.

Michno, Greg. "Lakota Noon at Greasy Grass." *Wild West,* June 1996. http://www.thehistorynet.com/we/html.

Mishkin, Bernard. *Rank & Warfare Among the Plains Indians.* Lincoln, NE: University of Nebraska Press, 1940.

Moses, L.G., and Wilson, Raymond, Eds. *Indian Lives: Essays on Nineteenth- and Twentieth-Century Native American Leaders.* Albuquerque: University of New Mexico Press, 1985.

Nagler, Barney. *The American Horse.* New York: The Macmillan Company, 1966.

Nelson, Bruce. *Land of the Dakotahs.* Lincoln, NE: University of Nebraska Press, 1946.

Norris, Kathleen. *Dakota: A Spiritual Geography.* New York: Houghton Mifflin Company, 1993.

Nurge, Ethel. *The Modern Sioux: Social Systems and Reservation Culture.* Lincoln, NE: University of Nebraska Press, 1970.

Paige, Harry W., PhD *Songs of the Teton Sioux.* Los Angeles: Westernlore Press, 1970.

Percheron Horse Association of America. Fredericktown, OH. http://www.geocities.com/phaoa/aboutus.htm.

Rice, Earle Jr. *The World History Series: The Battle of the Little Bighorn.* San Diego: Lucent Books, 1998.

Roe, Frank Gilbert. *The Indian and the Horse.* Norman, OK: University of Oklahoma Press, 1955.

Sandoz, Mari. *The Battle of the Little Bighorn.* Lincoln, NE: University of Nebraska Press, 1978.

Standing Bear, Luther. *My Indian Boyhood.* Lincoln, NE: University of Nebraska Press, 1931.

_____. *Stories of the Sioux.* Lincoln, NE: University of Nebraska Press, 1934.

_____. "A First Buffalo Hunt," in *Eyewitness to the American West: From the Aztec Empire to the Digital Frontier in the Words of Those Who Saw It Happen,* edited by David Colbert. New York: Viking, 1998.

Taylor, Colin F. *Sun'ka Wakan: Sacred Horses of the Plains.* Wyk auf Foehr, Germany: Verlag fuer Amerikanistik, 1995.

United States Census Bureau. *Census 2000, Special Tabulations.* U.S. Dept. of Commerce.

Vernam, Glenn R. *Man on Horseback.* Lincoln, NE: University of Nebraska Press, 1964.

Walker, James. *Lakota Society.* Lincoln, NE: University of Nebraska Press, 1982.

West, Ian. "Tributes to a Horse Nation: Plains Indian Horse Effigies." *South Dakota History, South Dakota State Historical Society and Board of Cultural Preservation Quarterly* 9, no. 4 (1979): 291-302.

# Reprint Acknowledgments

Grateful acknowledgment is made to the following for permission to reprint previously published material:

"A Cowboy's Prayer," Badger Clark, *Sun and Saddle Leather*. (Boston: The Gorham Press, 1922).

"Big Foot Riders Song," Wilmer Mesteth, 1988. *Porcupine and Brotherhood Singers: Remembering the Singer, Vol. 7*. © 1995 by Canyon Records Productions. Reprinted by permission of Canyon Records Productions.

"He's an Indian Cowboy in the Rodeo," Buffy Sainte-Marie. *Moonshot*. © 1972 by Buffy Sainte-Marie and Gypsy Boy Music, Inc. Reprinted by permission of Buffy Sainte-Marie.

"Many Horses Die in Snow Winter," Gerald Hausman. *Meditations with Animals: A Native American Bestiary*. © 1986 by Inner Traditions, Bear & Co. Reprinted by permission of Inner Traditions, Bear & Co.

"My Horse," Lone Man from *Teton Sioux Music and Culture* by Frances Densmore. © 1992 University of Nebraska Press.

"Reminiscences of William Darnell," George A. Root. © *Kansas Historical Collections, 1926-1928*, 17 (1928) 507, Reprinted by permission of the Kansas State Historical Society.

"Reservation Cowboy," Buddy Red Bow. *Black Hills Dreamer*. © 1991 Tatanka Records, Etherean Music, Inc. www.ethereanmusic.com. Reprinted by permission of Etherean Music, Inc.

"They Will Appear" from *In the Trail of the Wind: American Indian Poems and Ritual Orations*, edited by John Bierhorst. © 1971, renewed 2000 by John Bierhorst. Reprinted by permission of Farrar, Straus and Giroux, LLC.

"When a Horse Neighs," Brave Bull from *Teton Sioux Music and Culture* by Frances Densmore. © 1992 University of Nebraska Press.